Reminiscences of Captain Gronow

Rees Howell Gronow

Contents

REMINISCENCES OF CAPTAIN GRONOW

BY

Rees Howell Gronow

EDITOR'S NOTE

The spelling in this book is rather creative (including the occasional spelling of "ankle" as "ancle"), and the punctuation is remarkably varied. I have tried to preserve both, except that the spaces between a word and the following colon or semicolon have been removed. There are also many French words and phrases, whose meaning will usually be obvious as soon as you realise they are French. Of course I apologize for any genuine errors in spelling and punctuation that have crept into this file.

Captain Gronow is an entertaining raconteur who brings his own experiences in the Regency period and the wars with France delightfully to life. Gronow published several sets of memoirs. This file covers the first half of what he published. Search the web for "Captain Gronow" to learn more about this interesting gentleman.

The text is arranged as a series of topics, each with a title in capital letters. Sometimes there is continuity in this arrangement, sometimes there is not. There is no other structure to the text.

I have used the character for "pounds" (money) in this text: 'L'. If the character in single quotes does not look like a pound sign to you, well, at least you know what is intended. The book text uses a lower case 'l' for this purpose, but in computer fonts the 'l', looking just like a '1' when following a string of digits, is confusing.

Many thanks to Pam Wisniewski for proofreading this text.

--Tobias D. Robison, September, 2001

Reminiscences of Captain Gronow

Formerly of the Grenadier Guards, and M.P. for Stafford:

being

Anecdotes of the camp, the court, and the clubs, at the close of the last war with France.

Related by himself.

"O friends regretted, scenes for ever dear!
Remembrance hails you with her warmest tear!
Drooping she bends o'er pensive fancy's urn,
To trace the hours which never can return."

London:
Smith, Elder and Co., 65, Cornhill.
M.DCCC.LXII.

A FEW WORDS TO THE READER

It has been my lot to have lived through the greater part of one of the most eventful centuries of England's history, and I have been thrown amongst most of the remarkable men of my day; whether soldiers, statesman, men of letters, theatrical people, or those whose birth and fortune--rather, perhaps, than their virtues or talents--have caused them to be conspicuous in society at home or abroad. Nature having endowed me with a strong memory, I can recall with all their original vividness scenes that took place fifty years ago, and distinctly recollect the face, walk, and voice, as well as the dress and general manner, of everyone whom I have known. I have frequently repeated to my friends what I have seen and heard since the year that I joined the Guards (1813), and have been urged to commit to paper my anecdotes and reminiscences.

Unfortunately, I have not the power of efficiently describing in words the pictures that are hung up in the long gallery of my memory: a man may see very distinctly the landscape before him, yet he may be unable to delineate that which he gazes upon and is intimately acquainted with. A viva voce narrative of an incident told to a friend in conversation may pass muster, and one is able to fill up any gaps in an imperfect description; but it always occurred to me that I had no right to task a reader's time and patience unless I could put before him what I had to say in a lucid and complete form; I therefore refrained from committing myself to print. I have at length, however, yielded to the suggestion of friends, and written down some anecdotes in the best way I could. Soldiers are not generally famous for literary excellence, and when I was young, the military man was, perhaps, much less a scholar than he is at the present day; but I hope that the interest of the matter will make up for any deficiency of style.

In going over more than half a century, and treating of men, women and events, it was necessary to leave out many anecdotes which would, perhaps, have been more interesting than most of those that I have given; for I would not willingly offend, or hurt the feelings of any one, and I wish to respect the memory of the dead, as well as to take into consideration the sensitiveness of the living. My Reminiscences, it will be seen, are nothing more than miniature illustrations of contemporary history; and though the reader may find here and there scraps of biographical matter, I confine myself to facts and characteristics which were familiar to the circle in which I moved, and perhaps are as much public property as the painted portraits of celebrities.

Should this work meet with the approbation of the public, I hope at a future time to publish an additional one, as my memory still serves me with sufficient materials for another volume of a similar kind.

R. H. Gronow.

MY ENTRANCE INTO THE ARMY

After leaving Eton, I received an Ensign's commission in the First Guards during the month of December, 1812. Though many years have elapsed, I still remember my boyish delight at being named to so distinguished a regiment, and at the prospect of soon taking a part in the glorious deeds of our army in Spain. I joined in February 1813, and cannot but recollect with astonishment how limited and imperfect was the instruction which an officer received at that time: he absolutely entered the army without any military education whatever. We were so defective in our drill, even after we had passed out of the hands of the sergeant, that the excellence of our non-commissioned officers alone prevented us from meeting with the most fatal disasters in the face of the enemy. Physical force and our bull-dog energy carried many a hard-fought field. Luckily, nous avons change tout cela, and our officers may now vie with those of any other army in an age when the great improvements in musketry, in artillery practice, and in the greater rapidity of manoeuvring, have entirely changed the art of war, and rendered the individual education of those in every grade of command an absolute necessity.

After passing through the hands of the drill sergeant with my friends Dashwood, Batty, Browne, Lascelles, Hume, and Masters, and mounting guard at St. James's for a few months, we were hurried off, one fine morning, in charge of a splendid detachment of five hundred men to join Lord Wellington in Spain. Macadam had just begun to do for England what Marshal Wade did in Scotland seventy years before; and we were able to march twenty miles a day with ease until we reached Portsmouth. There we found transports ready to convey a large reinforcement, of which we formed part, to Lord Wellington, who was now making his arrangements, after taking St. Sebastian, for a yet more important event in the history of the Peninsular War--the invasion of France.

DEPARTURE FOR AND ARRIVAL IN SPAIN

We sailed under convoy of the Madagascar frigate, commanded by Captain Curtis; and, after a favourable voyage, we arrived at Passages. Our stay there was short, for we were ordered to join the army without loss of time. In three hours we got fairly into camp, where we were received with loud cheers by our brothers in arms.

The whole British army was here under canvas; our allies, the Spaniards and Portuguese, being in the rear. About the middle of October, to our great delight, the army received orders to cross the Bidassoa. At three o'clock on the morning of the 15th our regiment advanced through a difficult country, and, after a harassing march, reached the top of a hill as the gray light of morning began to dawn. We marched in profound silence, but with a pleasurable feeling of excitement amongst all ranks at the thought of meeting the enemy, and perhaps with not an equally agreeable idea that we might be in the next world before the day was over.

As we ascended the rugged side of the hill, I saw, for the first time, the immortal Wellington. He was accompanied by the Spanish General, Alava, Lord Fitzroy Somerset, and Major, afterwards Colonel Freemantle. He was very stern and grave-looking; he was in deep meditation, so long as I kept him in view, and spoke to no one. His features were bold, and I saw much decision of character in his expression. He rode a knowing-looking, thorough-bred horse, and wore a gray overcoat, Hessian boots, and a large cocked hat. We commenced the passage of the Bidassoa about five in the morning, and in a short time infantry, cavalry, and artillery found themselves upon French ground. The stream at the point we forded was nearly four feet deep, and had Soult been aware of what we were about, we should have found the passage of the river a very arduous undertaking.

Three miles above, we discovered the French army, and ere long found ourselves under fire. The sensation of being made a target to a large body of men is at first not particularly pleasant, but "in a trice, the ear becomes more Irish and less nice." The first man I ever saw killed was a Spanish soldier, who was cut in two by a cannon ball. The French army, not long after we began to return their fire, was in full retreat; and after a little sharp, but desultory fighting, in which our Division met with some loss, we took possession of the camp and strong position of Soult's army. We found the soldiers' huts very comfortable; they were built of branches of trees and furze, and formed squares and streets, which had names placarded up, such as Rue de Paris, Rue de Versailles, &c. We were not sorry to find ourselves in such commodious quarters, as well as being well housed. The scenery surrounding the camp was picturesque and grand. From our elevated position, immediately in front, we commanded a wide and extensive plain, intersected by two important rivers, the Nive and the Nivelle. On the right, the lofty Pyrenees, with their grand and varied outline, stood forth conspicuously in a blue, cloudless sky; on our left was the Bay of Biscay, with our cruisers perpetually on the move.

We witnessed from the camp, one night about twelve o'clock, a fight at sea, between an English brig and a French corvette, which was leaving the Adour with provisions and ammunition. She was chased by the brig, and brought to action. The night was sufficiently clear to enable us to discover distinctly the position of the vessels and the measured flash of their guns. They were at close quarters, and in less than half an hour we discovered the crew of the corvette taking to their boats. Shortly afterwards the vessel blew up with a loud explosion. We came to the conclusion that sea-fighting was more agreeable than land-fighting, as the crews of the vessels engaged without previous heavy marching, and with loose light clothing; there was no manoeuvring or standing for hours on the defensive; the wounded were immediately taken below and attended to, and the whole affair was over in a pleasingly brief period.

THE UNIFORM AND BEARING OF THE FRENCH SOLDIER

The French infantry soldier averaged about five feet five or six in height; in build they were much about what they are now, perhaps a little broader over the shoulder. They were smart, active, handy fellows, and much more able to look after their personal comforts than British soldiers, as their camps indicated. The uniform of those days consisted in a schako, which spread out at the top; a short-waisted, swallow-tailed coat; and large, baggy trousers and gaiters. The clothing of the French soldier was roomy, and enabled him to march and move about at ease: no pipeclay accessories occupied their attention; in a word, their uniforms and accoutrements were infinitely superior to our own, taking into consideration the practical necessities of warfare. Their muskets were inferior to ours, and their firing less deadly. The French cavalry we thought badly horsed; but their uniforms, though showy, were, like those of the infantry, comfortably large and roomy.

I have frequently remarked that firearms are of little use to the mounted soldier, and often an incumbrance to man and horse. Cavalry want only one arm--the sabre. Let the men be well mounted and at home in the saddle. It requires great knowledge in a Commander-in-chief to know when and how to use his cavalry. It has been my misfortune to witness oft-repeated blunders in the employment of the best-mounted regiments in the world. I consider the French generals had more knowledge of the use of cavalry than our own, when a great battle was to be fought.

MAJOR-GENERAL STEWART AND LORD WELLINGTON

If the present generation of Englishmen would take the trouble of looking at the newspaper which fifty years ago informed the British public of passing events both at home and abroad, they would, doubtless, marvel at the very limited and imperfect amount of intelligence which the best journals were enabled to place before their readers. The progress of the Peninsular campaign was very imperfectly chronicled; it will, therefore, be easily imagined what interest was attached to certain letters that appeared in the Morning Chronicle which criticised with much severity, and frequently with considerable injustice, the military movements of Lord Wellington's Spanish campaign.

The attention of the Commander-in-Chief being drawn to these periodical and personal comments on his conduct of the war, his lordship at once perceived from the information which they contained that they must have been written by an officer holding a high command under him. Determined to ascertain the author--who, in addressing a public journal, was violating the Articles of War, and, it might be, assisting the enemy--means were employed in London to identify the writer. The result was, that Lord Wellington discovered the author of the letters to be no other than Sir Charles Stewart, the late Lord Londonderry. As soon as Lord Wellington had made himself master of this fact, he summoned Sir Charles Stewart to headquarters at Torres Vedras; and on his appearance, he, without the least preface, addressed him thus:--

"Charles Stewart, I have ascertained with deep regret that you are the author of the letters which appeared in the Morning Chronicle abusing me and finding fault with my military plans."

Lord Wellington paused here for a moment, and then continued:

"Now, Stewart, you know your brother Castlereagh is my best friend, to whom I owe everything; nevertheless, if you continue to write letters to the Chronicle, or any other newspaper, by God, I will send you home."

Sir Charles Stewart was so affected at this rebuke that he shed tears, and expressed himself deeply penitent for the breach of confidence and want of respect for the Articles of War. They immediately shook hands and parted friends. It happened, however, that Sir Charles Stewart did not remain long in the cavalry, of which he was Adjutant-General. Within a few weeks he was named one of the Commissioners deputed to proceed to the Allied Armies, where the Sovereigns were then completing their plans to crush Napoleon.

ST. JEAN DE LUZ

During the winter of 1813, the Guards were stationed with head-quarters at St Jean de Luz, and most comfortable we managed to make them. For some short time previously we had been on scanty commons, and had undergone considerable privation: indeed we might have said, like the Colonel to Johnny Newcome on his arrival to join his regiment, "We sons of Mars have long been fed on brandy and cigars." I had no cause to complain personally; for my servant, a Sicilian, was one of the most accomplished foragers (ill-natured persons might give him a worse name) in the whole army; and when others were nearly starving, he always managed to provide meat or poultry. He rode on his mule sometimes from twenty to thirty miles, often running the greatest dangers, to procure me a good meal; of which he took care to have, very justly, a large share for himself.

At St Jean de Luz, we were more attentive to our devotions than we had been for some time. Divine service was performed punctually every Sunday on the sand-hills near the town; Lord Wellington and his numerous Staff placed themselves in the midst of our square, and his lordship's chaplain read the service, to which Lord Wellington always appeared to listen with great attention.

The mayor of the town, thinking to please "the great English lord," gave a ball at the Hotel de Ville: our Commander-in-Chief did not go but was represented by Waters. I was there, and expected to see some of the young ladies of the country so famed for their beauty; they were, however, far too patriotic to appear, and the only lady present was Lady Waldegrave, then living with her husband at head-quarters. What was one partner among so many? The ball was a dead failure, in spite of the efforts of the mayor, who danced, to our intense amusement, an English hornpipe, which he had learnt in not a very agreeable manner, viz. when a prisoner of war in the hulks at Plymouth.

There were two packs of hounds at St Jean de Luz; one kept by Lord Wellington, the other by Marsden, of the Commissariat: our officers went uncommonly straight. Perhaps our best man across country (though sometimes somewhat against his will) was the late Colonel Lascelles of my regiment, then, like myself, a mere lad. He rode a horse seventeen hands high, called Bucephalus, which invariably ran away with him, and more than once had nearly capsized Lord Wellington. The good living at St Jean de Luz agreed so well with my friend that he waxed fat, and from that period to his death was known to the world by the jovial appellation of Bacchus Lascelles.

Shortly before we left St Jean de Luz, we took our turn of outposts in the neighbourhood of Bidart, a large village, about ten miles from Bayonne. Early one frosty morning in December, an order came, that if we saw the enemy advancing, we were not to fire or give the alarm. About five, we perceived two battalions wearing grenadier caps coming on. They turned out to belong to a Nassau regiment which had occupied the advanced post of the enemy, and, hearing that Napoleon had met with great reverses in Germany, signified to us their intention to desert. They were a fine-looking body of men, and appeared, I thought, rather ashamed of the step they had taken. On the same day, we were relieved, and on our way back met Lord Wellington with his hounds. He was dressed in a light blue frock coat (the colour of the Hatfield hunt) which had been sent out to him as a present from Lady Salisbury, then one of the leaders of the fashionable world, and an enthusiastic admirer of his lordship.

Here, I remember seeing for the first time a very remarkable character, the Hon. W. Dawson, of my regiment. He was surrounded by muleteers, with whom he was bargaining to provide carriage for innumerable hampers of wine, liqueurs, hams, potted meat, and other good things, which he had brought from England. He was a particularly gentlemanly and amiable man, much beloved by the regiment: no one was so hospitable or lived so magnificently. His cooks were the best in the army, and he, besides, had a host of servants of all nations--Spaniards, French, Portuguese, Italians--who were employed in scouring the country for provisions. Lord Wellington once honoured him with his company; and on entering the ensign's tent, found him alone at table, with a dinner fit for a king, his plate and linen in good keeping, and his wines perfect. Lord Wellington was accompanied on this occasion by Sir Edward Pakenham and Colonel du Burgh, afterwards Lord Downes. It fell to my lot to partake of his princely hospitality and dine with him at his quarters, a farmhouse in a village on the Bidassoa, and I never saw a better dinner put upon table. The career of this amiable Amphitryon, to our great regret, was cut short, after exercising for about a year a splendid but not very wise hospitality. He had only a younger brother's fortune; his debts became very considerable, and he was obliged to quit the Guards. He and his friends had literally eaten up his little fortune.

FOOLHARDINESS

I may here recount an instance of the folly and foolhardiness of youth, and the recklessness to which a long course of exposure to danger produces. When Bayonne was invested, I was one night on duty on the outer picket. The ground inside the breastwork which had been thrown up for our protection by Burgoyne was in a most disagreeable state for any one who wished to repose after the fatigues of the day, being knee-deep in mud of a remarkably plastic nature. I was dead tired, and determined to get a little rest in some more agreeable spot; so calling my sergeant, I told him to give me his knapsack for a pillow; I would make a comfortable night of it on the top of the breastwork, as it was an invitingly dry place. "For heaven's sake take care, sir," said he; "you'll have fifty bullets in you: you will be killed to a certainty." "Pooh, nonsense," said I, and climbing up, I wrapt myself in my cloak, laid my head on the knapsack, and soon fell into a sound sleep.

By the mercy of Providence I remained in a whole skin, either from the French immediately underneath not perceiving me, or not thinking me worth a shot; but when General Stopford came up with Lord James Hay (who not long since reminded me of this youthful escapade) I received a severe wigging, and was told to consider myself lucky that I was not put under arrest for exposing my life in so foolish a manner.

Among the many officers of the Guards who were taken prisoners in the unfortunate sortie from Bayonne, was the Hon. H. Townshend, commonly called Bull Townshend. He was celebrated as a bon vivant, and in consequence of his too great indulgence in the pleasures of the table, had become very unwieldy and could not move quick enough to please his nimble captors, so he received many prods in the back from a sharp bayonet. After repeated threats, however, he was dismissed with what our American friends would be pleased to designate "a severe booting." The late Sir Willoughby Cotton was also a prisoner. It really seemed as if the enemy had made choice of our fattest officers. Sir Willoughby escaped by giving up his watch and all the money which he had in his pockets; but this consisting of a Spanish dollar only, the smallness of the sum subjected him to the same ignominious treatment as had been experienced by Townshend.

Among the numerous bad characters in our ranks, several were coiners, or utterers of bad money. In the second brigade of Guards, just before we arrived at St. Jean de Luz, a soldier was convicted of this offence, and was sentenced to receive 800 lashes. This man made sham Spanish dollars out of the pewter spoons of the regiment. As he had before been convicted and flogged, he received this terrible sentence, and died under the lash. Would it not have been better to have condemned him to be shot?-- It would have been more humane, certainly more military, and far less brutal.

DISCIPLINE

When the headquarters of the army were at St Jean de Luz, Soult made a movement in front of our right centre, which the English general took for a reconnaissance. As the French general perceived that we had ordered preparations to receive him, he sent a flag of truce to demand a cessation of hostilities, saying that he wanted to shoot an officer and several men for acts of robbery committed by them, with every sort of atrocity, on the farmers and peasantry of the country. The execution took place in view of both armies, and a terrible lesson it was. I cannot specify the date of this event, but think it must have been the latter end of November, 1813. About the same time General Harispe, who commanded a corps of Basques, issued a proclamation forbidding the peasantry to supply the English with provisions or forage, on pain of death; it stated that we were savages, and, as a proof of this, our horses were born with short tails. I saw this absurd proclamation, which was published in French and in the Basque languages, and distributed all over the country. Before we left the neighbourhood of Bayonne for Bordeaux, a soldier was hanged for robbery, on the sands of the Adour. This sort of punishment astonished the French almost as much as it did the soldier. On a march we were very severe, and if any of our men were caught committing an act of violence or brigandage, the offender was tried by a drum-head court-martial, and hanged in a very short time.

I knew an officer of the 18th Hussars, W. R., young, rich, and a fine-looking fellow, who joined the army not far from St Sebastian. His stud of horses was remarkable for their blood, his grooms were English, and three in number. He brought with him a light cart to carry forage, and a fourgon for his own baggage. All went on well, till he came to go on outpost duty; but not finding there any of the comforts to which he had been accustomed, he quietly mounted his charger, told his astonished sergeant that campaigning was not intended for a gentleman, and instantly galloped off to his quarters, ordering his servants to pack up everything immediately, as he had hired a transport to take him off to England. He left us before any one had time to stop him; and though despatches were sent off to the Commander-in-Chief, requesting that a court-martial might sit to try the young deserter, he arrived home long enough before the despatches to enable him to sell out of his regiment. He deserved to have been shot.

Sir John Hope, who commanded our corps d'armee at Bayonne, had his quarters at a village on the Adour, called Beaucauld. He was good enough to name me to the command of the village; which honour I did not hold for many days, for the famous sortie from Bayonne took place soon after, and the general was made prisoner.

SIR JOHN WATERS

Amongst the distinguished men in the Peninsular war whom my memory brings occasionally before me, is the well-known and highly popular Quartermaster General Sir John Waters, who was born at Margam, a Welsh village in Glamorganshire. He was one of those extraordinary persons that seem created by kind nature for particular purposes; and, without using the word in an offensive sense, he was the most admirable spy that was ever attached to an army. One would almost have thought that the Spanish war was entered upon and carried on in order to display his remarkable qualities. He could assume the character of Spaniards of every degree and station, so as to deceive the most acute of those whom he delighted to imitate. In the posada of the village he was hailed by the contrabandist or the muleteer as one of their own race; in the gay assemblies he was an accomplished hidalgo; at the bull-fight the toreador received his congratulations as from one who had encountered the toro in the arena; in the church he would converse with the friar upon the number of Ave Marias and Pater-nosters which could lay a ghost, or tell him the history of everyone who had perished by the flame of the Inquisition, relating his crime, whether carnal or anti-Catholic; and he could join in the seguadilla or in the guaracha. But what rendered him more efficient than all was his wonderful power of observation and accurate description, which made the information he gave so reliable and valuable to the Duke of Wellington. Nothing escaped him. When amidst a group of persons, he would minutely watch the movement, attitude, and expression of every individual that composed it; in the scenery by which he was surrounded he would carefully mark every object:--not a tree, not a bush, not a large stone, escaped his observation; and it was said that in a cottage he noted every piece of crockery on the shelf, every domestic utensil, and even the number of knives and forks that were got ready for use at dinner. His acquaintance with the Spanish language was marvellous; from the finest works of Calderon to the ballads in the patois of every province, he could quote, to the infinite delight of those with whom he associated. He could assume any character that he pleased: he could be the Castilian, haughty and reserved; the Asturian, stupid and plodding; the

Catalonian, intriguing and cunning; the Andalusian, laughing and merry;--in short, he was all things to all men. Nor was he incapable of passing off, when occasion required, for a Frenchman; but as he spoke the language with a strong German accent, he called himself an Alsatian. He maintained that character with the utmost nicety; and as there is a strong feeling of fellowship, almost equal to that which exists in Scotland, amongst all those who are born in the departments of France bordering on the Rhine, and who maintain their Teutonic originality, he always found friends and supporters in every regiment in the French service.

He was on one occasion entrusted with a very difficult mission by the Duke of Wellington, which he undertook effectually to perform, and to return on a particular day with the information that was required.

Great was the disappointment when it was ascertained beyond a doubt that just after leaving the camp he had been taken prisoner, before he had time to exchange his uniform. Such, however, was the case: a troop of dragoons had intercepted him, and carried him off; and the commanding officer desired two soldiers to keep a strict watch over him and carry him to head-quarters. He was of course disarmed, and being placed on a horse, was, after a short time, galloped off by his guards. He slept one night under durance vile at a small inn, where he was allowed to remain in the kitchen; conversation flowed on very glibly, and as he appeared a stupid Englishman, who could not understand a word of French or Spanish, he was allowed to listen, and thus obtained precisely the intelligence that he was in search of. The following morning, being again mounted, he overheard a conversation between his guards, who deliberately agreed to rob him, and to shoot him at a mill where they were to stop, and to report to their officer that they had been compelled to fire at him in consequence of his attempt to escape.

Shortly before they arrived at the mill, for fear that they might meet with some one who would insist on having a portion of the spoil, the dragoons took from the prisoner his watch and his purse, which he surrendered with a good grace. On their arrival at the mill, they dismounted, and in order to give some appearance of truth to their story, they went into the house; leaving their prisoner outside, in the hope that he would make some attempt to escape. In an instant Waters threw his cloak upon a neighbouring olive bush, and mounted his cocked hat on the top. Some empty flour sacks lay upon the ground, and a horse laden with well-filled flour sacks stood at the door. Sir John contrived to enter one of the empty sacks and throw himself across the horse. When the soldiers came out of the house they fired their carbines at the supposed prisoner, and galloped off at their utmost speed.

A short time after the miller came out and mounted his steed; the general contrived to rid himself of the encumbrance of the sack, and sat up, riding behind the man, who, suddenly turning round, saw a ghost, as he believed, for the flour that still remained in the sack had completely whitened his fellow-traveller and given him a most unearthly appearance. The frightened miller was "putrified," as Mrs. Malaprop would say, at the sight, and a push from the white spectre brought the unfortunate man to the ground, when away rode the gallant quartermaster with his sacks of flour, which, at length bursting, made a ludicrous spectacle of man and horse.

On reaching the English camp, where Lord Wellington was anxiously deploring his fate, a sudden shout from the soldiers made his lordship turn round, when a figure, resembling the statue in "Don Juan," galloped up to him. The duke, affectionately shaking him by the hand, said--

"Waters, you never yet deceived me; and though you have come in a most questionable shape, I must congratulate you and myself."

When this story was told at the clubs, one of those listeners, who always want something more, called out, "Well, and what did Waters say?" to which Alvanley replied--

"Oh, Waters made a very flowery speech, like a well-bred man."

THE BATTLE OF THE NIVELLE

We expected to remain quietly in our winter quarters at St. Jean de Luz; but, to our surprise, early one morning, we were aroused from sleep by the beating of the drum calling us to arms. We were soon in marching order. It appeared that our outposts had been severely pushed by the French, and we were called upon to support our companions in arms.

The whole of the British army, as well as the division of the Guards, had commenced a forward movement. Soult, seeing this, entirely changed his tactics, and from that time, viz. the 9th of December, a series of engagements took place. The fighting on the 9th was comparatively insignificant. When we were attacked on the 10th, the Guards held the mayor's house, and the grounds and orchards attached: this was an important station.

Large bodies of the enemy's infantry approached, and, after desultory fighting, succeeded in penetrating our position, when many hand-to-hand combats ensued. Towards the afternoon, officers and men having displayed great gallantry, we drove the enemy from the ground which they courageously disputed with us, and from which they eventually retreated to Bayonne. Every day there was constant fighting along the whole of our line, which extended from the sea to the lower Pyrenees--a distance probably not less than thirty miles.

On the 11th, we only exchanged a few shots, but on the 12th Soult brought into action from fifteen to twenty thousand men, and attacked our left with a view of breaking our line. One of the most remarkable incidents of the 12th was the fact of an English battalion being surrounded by a division of French in the neighbourhood of the mayor's house--which, as before observed, was one of our principal strategical positions. The French commanding officer, believing that no attempt would be made to resist, galloped up to the officer of the British regiment, and demanded his sword. Upon this, without the least hesitation, the British officer shouted out, "This fellow wants us to surrender: charge, my boys! and show them what stuff we are made of." Instantaneously, a hearty cheer rang out, and our men rushed forward impetuously, drove off the enemy at the point of the bayonet, and soon disposed of the surrounding masses. In a few minutes they had taken prisoners, or killed, the whole of the infantry regiment opposed to them.

On the 13th was fought the bloody battle of the Nivelle. Soult had determined to make a gigantic effort to drive us back into Spain. During the night of the 12th, he rapidly concentrated about sixty thousand troops in front of Sir Rowland Hill's corps d'armee, consisting of 15,000 men, who occupied a very strong position, which was defended by some of the best artillery in the world. At daybreak Sir Rowland Hill was astonished to find himself threatened by masses of infantry advancing over a country luckily intersected by rivulets, hedges, and woods, which prevented the enemy from making a rapid advance; whilst, at the same time, it was impossible on such ground to employ cavalry. Sir Rowland, availing himself of an elevated position, hurriedly surveyed his ground, and concentrated his men at such points as he knew the nature of the field would induce the enemy to attack. The French, confident of success from their superior numbers, came gallantly up, using the bayonet for the first time in a premeditated attack; Our men stood their ground, and for hours acted purely on the defensive; being sustained by the admirable practice of our artillery, whose movements no difficulty of ground could, on this occasion, impede, so efficiently were the guns horsed, and so perfect was the training of the officers. It was not until mid-day that the enemy became discouraged at finding that they were unable to make any serious impression on our position; they then retired in good order, Sir Rowland Hill not daring to follow them.

Lord Wellington arrived just in time to witness the end of the battle; and while going over the field with Sir Rowland Hill, he remarked that he had never seen so many men hors de combat in so small a space.

I must not omit to mention a circumstance which occurred during this great fight, alike illustrative of cowardice and of courage. The colonel of an infantry regiment, who shall be nameless, being hard pressed, showed a disposition not only to run away himself, but to order his regiment to retire. In fact, a retrograde movement had commenced, when my gallant and dear friend Lord Charles Spencer, aide-de-camp to Sir William Stewart, dashed forward, and, seizing the colours of the regiment, exclaimed, "If your colonel will not lead you, follow me, my boys." The gallantry of this youth, then only eighteen years of age, so animated the regiment, and restored their confidence, that they rallied and shared in the glory of the day.

THE PASSAGE OF THE ADOUR

Immediately after the battle of Nivelle, Lord Wellington determined to advance his whole line on to French ground. The right, under his own command, pushed on towards Orthes, whilst the left, under the command of Sir John Hope, proceeded in the direction of Bayonne. We (the Guards) were incorporated in the latter corps d'armee.

Whilst these operations were going on, Soult was organizing his discouraged army, in order to make, as early as possible, another convenient stand. The enemy fell back on Orthes, and there took up a strong position; Soult was, nevertheless, destined to be beaten again at Orthes. It so happened that, for the first time since the battle of Vittoria, our cavalry were engaged: the nature of the ground at Nive and Nivelle was such as to prevent the possibility of employing the mounted soldier.

I must here record an incident which created a considerable sensation in military circles in connection with the battle of Orthes. The 10th Hussars, officered exclusively by men belonging to the noblest families of Great Britain, showed a desire to take a more active part in the contest than their colonel (Quintin) thought prudent. They pressed hard to be permitted to charge the French cavalry on more than one occasion, but in vain. This so disgusted every officer in the regiment, that they eventually signed a round robin, by which they agreed never again to speak to their colonel. When the regiment returned to England, a court of inquiry was held, which resulted, through the protection of the Prince Regent, in the colonel's exoneration from all blame, and at the same time the exchange of the rebellious officers into other regiments.

It was at the battle of Orthes that the late Duke of Richmond was shot through the body, gallantly fighting with the 7th Fusiliers. Lord Wellington had determined to cross the Adour, and Sir John Hope was intrusted with a corps d'armee, which was the first to perform this difficult operation. It was necessary to provide Sir John Hope with a number of small boats; these were accordingly brought on the backs of mules from various Spanish ports, it being impossible, on account of the surf at the entrance of the Adour, as well as the command which the French held of that river, for Lord Wellington to avail himself of water carriage. Soult had given orders for the forces under General Thevenot to dispute the passage.

The first operations of our corps were to throw over the 3rd Guards, under the command of the gallant Colonel Stopford; this was not accomplished without much difficulty: but it was imperatively necessary, in order to protect the point where the construction of the bridge of boats would terminate. They had not been long on the French side of the river before a considerable body of men were seen issuing from Bayonne. Sir John Hope ordered our artillery, and rockets, then for the first time employed, to support our small band. Three or four regiments of French infantry were approaching rapidly, when a well-directed fire of rockets fell amongst them. The consternation of the Frenchmen was such, when these hissing, serpent-like projectiles descended, that a panic ensued, and they retreated upon Bayonne. The next day the bridge of boats was completed, and the whole army crossed. Bayonne was eventually invested after a contest, in which it was supposed our loss exceeded 500 or 600 men. Here we remained in camp about six weeks, expecting to besiege the citadel; but this event never came off: we, however, met with a severe disaster and a reverse. The enemy made an unexpected sortie, and surrounded General Sir John Hope, when he and the whole of his staff were taken prisoners. The French killed and wounded about 1,000 men on this occasion.

The hardly-contested battle of Toulouse was fought about this period, but the Guards were not present to share the honours of a contest which closed the eventful war of the Spanish Peninsula.

ARRIVAL OF THE GUARDS AT BORDEAUX

When we reached Bordeaux, which had now become a stronghold of the Royalists, we were received by the inhabitants with a welcome which resembled what would be shown to friends and deliverers, rather than to a foreign soldiery. Nothing could be more gratifying and more acceptable to our feelings, since it was the first time after our arrival on the Continent that we met with cordiality and an apparent desire to make our quarters as comfortable as possible. The Duc d'Angouleme had reached Bordeaux before us, and no doubt his presence had prepared the way for all the friends of the Bourbons. Everywhere some description of white rag was doing duty for a Royalist banner. I lived at M. Devigne's, a rich wine-merchant who had a family of two sons and two beautiful daughters; the latter were, as I thought, taken remarkable care of by their maternal parent. Here I had evidently fallen upon my legs, for not only was the family a most agreeable one, but their hospitality was of the most generous kind. Sir Stapylton Cotton was our frequent visitor, together with M. Martignac, afterwards Minister of Charles the Tenth.

Here I had an opportunity of meeting some of the prettiest women of a city famed all over Europe for its female beauty. The young ladies were remarkable for their taste in dress, which in those days consisted of a mantilla a l'Espagnole, and silken shawls of varied hues, so admirably blended, that the eye was charmed with their richness of colour. The grisettes, who were as much admired by the soldiers as were the high dames by the officers, were remarkable for a coquettish species of apron of a red dye, which was only to be obtained from the neighbourhood.

Of course we were all very anxious to taste the Bordeaux wines; but our palates, accustomed to the stronger vintages of Spain, I suspect were not in a condition to appreciate the more delicate and refined bouquets which ought to characterize claret. A vin ordinaire, which now at restaurateur's would cost three francs, was then furnished at the hotels for fifteen sous: a Larose, Lafitte, Margot, such as we are now paying eight or ten francs a bottle for, did not cost a third. I must not, however, forget that greater attention and care is now employed in the preparation of French wines. The exportation to England of the light red wines of France was not sufficiently profitable, as I learnt from my host, at that time to attract the cupidity of commerce.

In the Guards, Bordeaux was more affectionately remembered in connexion with its women than its wine. We left it with regret, and the more youthful and imaginative amongst us said that we were wafted across the Channel by the gentle sighs of the girls we left behind us.

MRS. MARY ANNE CLARKE

Our army, despite its defects, was nevertheless infinitely better administered at home when I joined than it had been a few years before; owing principally to the inquiry that had taken place in the House of Commons, relative to the bribery and corruption which had crept in, and which had been laid open by the confessions of a female, who created no small sensation in those days, and who eventually terminated her extraordinary career, not very long since, in Paris.

The squibs fired off by Mrs. Mary Anne Clarke had a much greater influence, and produced more effect upon the English army, than all the artillery of the enemy directed against the Duke of York when commanding in Holland. This lady was remarkable for her beauty and her fascinations; and few came within the circle over which she presided who did not acknowledge her superior power. Her wit, which kept the House of Commons, during her examination, in a continued state of merriment, was piquant and saucy. Her answers on that occasion have been so often brought before the public, that I need not repeat them; but, in private life, her quick repartee, and her brilliant sallies, rendered her a lively, though not always an agreeable companion. As for prudence, she had none; her dearest friend, if she had any, was just as likely to be made the object of her ridicule as the most obnoxious person of her acquaintance.

Her narrative of her first introduction to the Duke of York has often been repeated; but, as all her stories were considered apocryphal, it is difficult to arrive at a real history of her career. Certain however, is it that, about the age of sixteen, she was residing at Blackheath--a sweet, pretty, lively girl--when, in her daily walk across the heath, she was passed, on two or three occasions, by a handsome, well-dressed cavalier, who, finding that she recognised his salute, dismounted; pleased with her manner and wit, he begged to be allowed to introduce a friend. Accordingly, on her consenting, a person to whom the cavalier appeared to pay every sort of deference was presented to her, and the acquaintance ripened into something more than friendship. Not the slightest idea had the young lady of the position in society of her lover, until she accompanied him, on his invitation, to the theatre, where she occupied a private box, when she was surprised at the ceremony with which she was treated, and at observing that every eye and every lorgnette in the house were directed towards her in the course of the evening. She accepted this as a tribute to her beauty. Finding that she could go again to the theatre when she pleased, and occupy the same box, she availed herself of this opportunity with a female friend, and was not a little astonished at being addressed as Her Royal Highness. She then discovered that the individual into whose affections she had insinuated herself was the son of the King, the Duke of York, who had not long before united himself to a lady, for whom she had been mistaken.

Mrs. Mary Anne Clarke was soon reconciled to the thought of being the wife of a prince by the left hand, particularly as she found herself assiduously courted by persons of the highest rank, and more especially by military men. A large house in a fashionable street was taken for her, and an establishment on a magnificent scale gave her an opportunity of surrounding herself with persons of a sphere far beyond anything she could in her younger days have dreamt of; her father having been in an honourable trade, and her husband being only a captain in a marching regiment. The duke, delighted to see his fair friend so well received, constantly honoured her dinner-table with his presence, and willingly gratified any wish that she expressed; and he must have known (and for this he was afterwards highly censured) that her style of living was upon a scale of great expense, and that he himself contributed little towards it. The consequence was that the hospitable lady eventually became embarrassed, and knew not which way to turn to meet her outlay. It was suggested to her that she might obtain from the duke commissions in the army, which she could easily dispose of at a good price. Individuals quickly came forward, ready to purchase anything that came within her grasp, which she extended not only to the army, but, as it afterwards appeared, to the Church; for there were reverend personages who availed themselves of her assistance, and thus obtained patronage, by which they advanced their worldly interests very rapidly.

MRS. MARY ANNE CLARKE AND COL. WARDLE

Amongst those who paid great attention to Mrs. Mary Anne Clarke was Colonel Wardle, at that time a remarkable member of the House of Commons, and a bold leader of the Radical Opposition. He got intimately acquainted with her, and was so great a personal favourite that it was believed he wormed out all her secret history, of which he availed himself to obtain a fleeting popularity.

Having obtained the names of some of the parties who had been fortunate enough, as they imagined, to secure the lady's favour, he loudly demanded an inquiry in the House of Commons as to the management of the army by the Commander-in-Chief, the Duke of York. The nation and the army were fond of his Royal Highness, and every attempt to screen him was made; but in vain. The House undertook the task of investigating the conduct of the duke, and witnesses were produced, amongst whom was the fair lady herself, who by no means attempted to screen her imprudent admirer. Her responses to the questions put to her were cleverly and archly given, and the whole mystery of her various intrigues came to light. The duke consequently resigned his place in the Horse Guards, and at the same time repudiated the beautiful and dangerous cause of his humiliation. The lady, incensed at the desertion of her royal swain, announced her intention of publishing his love-letters, which were likely to expose the whole of the royal family to ridicule, as they formed the frequent themes of his correspondence. Sir Herbert Taylor was therefore commissioned to enter into a negotiation for the purchase of the letters; this he effected at an enormous price, obtaining a written document at the same time by which Mrs. Clarke was subjected to heavy penalties if she, by word or deed, implicated the honour of any of the branches of the royal family. A pension was secured to her, on condition that she should quit England, and reside wherever she chose on the Continent. To all this she consented, and, in the first instance, went to Brussels, where her previous history being scarcely known, she was well received; and she married her daughters without any inquiry as to the fathers to whom she might ascribe them.

Mrs. Clarke afterwards settled quietly and comfortably in Paris, receiving oc-casionally visits from members of the aristocracy who had known her when min-gling in a certain circle in London. The Marquis of Londonderry never failed to pay his respects to her, entertaining a very high opinion of her talents. Her manners were exceedingly agreeable, and to the latest day she retained pleasing traces of past beauty. She was lively, sprightly, and full of fun, and indulged in innumer-able anecdotes of the members of the royal family of England--some of them much too scandalous to be repeated. She regarded the Duke of York as a big baby, not out of his leading-strings, and the Prince of Wales as an idle sensualist, with just enough of brains to be guided by any laughing, well-bred individual who would listen to stale jokes and impudent ribaldry. Of Queen Charlotte she used to speak with the utmost disrespect, attributing to her a love of domination and a hatred of every one who would not bow down before any idol that she chose to set up; and as being envious of the Princess Caroline and her daughter the Princess Charlotte of Wales, and jealous of their acquiring too much influence over the Prince of Wales. In short, Mary Anne Clarke had been so intimately let into every secret of the life of the royal family that, had she not been tied down, her revelations would have astonished the world, however willing the people might have been to believe that they were tinged with scandal and exaggeration.

The way in which Colonel Wardle first obtained information of the sale of commissions was singular enough: he was paying a clandestine visit to Mrs. Clarke, when a carriage with the royal livery drove up to the door, and the gallant officer was compelled to take refuge under the sofa; but instead of the royal duke, there appeared one of his aide-de-camps, who entered into conversation in so mysterious a manner as to excite the attention of the gentleman under the sofa, and led him to believe that the sale of a commission was authorised by the Commander-in-Chief; though it afterwards appeared that it was a private arrangement of the unwelcome visitor. At the Horse-Guards, it had often been suspected that there was a mystery connected with commissions that could not be fathomed; as it frequently happened that the list of promotions agreed on was surreptitiously increased by the addition of new names. This was the crafty handiwork of the accomplished dame; the duke having employed her as his amanuensis, and being accustomed to sign her auto-graph lists without examination.

SOCIETY IN LONDON IN 1814

In the year 1814, my battalion of the Guards was once more in its old quarters in Portman Street barracks, enjoying the fame of our Spanish campaign. Good society at the period to which I refer was, to use a familiar expression, wonderfully "select." At the present time one can hardly conceive the importance which was attached to getting admission to Almack's, the seventh heaven of the fashionable world. Of the three hundred officers of the Foot Guards, not more than half a dozen were honoured with vouchers of admission to this exclusive temple of the beau monde; the gates of which were guarded by lady patronesses, whose smiles or frowns consigned men and women to happiness or despair. These lady patronesses were the Ladies Castlereagh, Jersey, Cowper, and Sefton, Mrs. Drummond Burrell, now Lady Willoughby, the Princess Esterhazy, and the Countess Lieven.

The most popular amongst these grandes dames was unquestionably Lady Cowper, now Lady Palmerston. Lady Jersey's bearing, on the contrary, was that of a theatrical tragedy queen; and whilst attempting the sublime, she frequently made herself simply ridiculous, being inconceivably rude, and in her manner often ill-bred. Lady Sefton was kind and amiable, Madame de Lieven haughty and exclusive, Princess Esterhazy was a bon enfant, Lady Castlereagh and Mrs. Burrell de tres grandes dames.

Many diplomatic arts, much finesse, and a host of intrigues, were set in motion to get an invitation to Almack's. Very often persons whose rank and fortunes entitled them to the entree anywhere, were excluded by the cliqueism of the lady patronesses; for the female government of Almack's was a pure despotism, and subject to all the caprices of despotic rule: it is needless to add that, like every other despotism, it was not innocent of abuses. The fair ladies who ruled supreme over this little dancing and gossiping world, issued a solemn proclamation that no gentleman should appear at the assemblies without being dressed in knee-breeches, white cravat, and chapeau bras. On one occasion, the Duke of Wellington was about to ascend the staircase of the ball-room, dressed in black trousers, when the vigilant Mr. Willis, the guardian of the establishment, stepped forward and said, "Your Grace cannot be admitted in trousers," whereupon the Duke, who had a great respect for orders and regulations, quietly walked away.

In 1814, the dances at Almack's were Scotch reels and the old English country-dance; and the orchestra, being from Edinburgh, was conducted by the then celebrated Neil Gow. It was not until 1815 that Lady Jersey introduced from Paris the favourite quadrille, which has so long remained popular. I recollect the persons who formed the very first quadrille that was ever danced at Almack's: they were Lady Jersey, Lady Harriet Butler, Lady Susan Ryder, and Miss Montgomery; the men being the Count St. Aldegonde, Mr. Montgomery, Mr. Montague, and Charles Standish. The "mazy waltz" was also brought to us about this time; but there were comparatively few who at first ventured to whirl round the salons of Almack's; in course of time Lord Palmerston might, however, have been seen describing an infinite number of circles with Madame de Lieven. Baron de Neumann was frequently seen perpetually turning with the Princess Esterhazy; and, in course of time, the waltzing mania, having turned the heads of society generally, descended to their feet, and the waltz was practised in the morning in certain noble mansions in London with unparalleled assiduity.

The dandies of society were Beau Brummell (of whom I shall have to say something on another occasion), the Duke of Argyle, the Lords Worcester, Alvanley, and Foley, Henry Pierrepoint, John Mills, Bradshaw, Henry de Ros, Charles Standish, Edward Montagu, Hervey Aston, Dan Mackinnon, George Dawson Damer, Lloyd (commonly known as Rufus Lloyd), and others who have escaped my memory. They were great frequenters of White's Club, in St. James's Street, where, in the famous bay window, they mustered in force.

Drinking and play were more universally indulged in then than at the present time, and many men still living must remember the couple of bottles of port at least which accompanied his dinner in those days. Indeed, female society amongst the upper classes was most notoriously neglected; except, perhaps, by romantic foreigners, who were the heroes of many at fashionable adventure that fed the clubs with ever acceptable scandal. How could it be otherwise, when husbands spent their days in the hunting-field, or were entirely occupied with politics, and always away from home during the day; whilst the dinner-party, commencing at seven or eight, frequently did not break up before one in the morning. There were then four-, and even five-bottle men; and the only thing that saved them was drinking very slowly, and out of very small glasses. The learned head of the law, Lord Eldon, and his brother, Lord Stowell, used to say that they had drunk more bad port than any two men in England; indeed, the former was rather apt to be overtaken, and to speak occasionally somewhat thicker than natural, after long and heavy potations. The late Lords Panmure, Dufferin, and Blayney, wonderful to relate, were six-bottle men at this time; and I really think that if the good society of 1815 could appear before their more moderate descendants in the state they were generally reduced to after dinner, the moderns would pronounce their ancestors fit for nothing but bed.

THE ITALIAN OPERA.--CATALANI

The greatest vocalist of whom I have a recollection, is Madame Catalani. In her youth, she was the finest singer in Europe, and she was much sought after by all the great people during her sejour in London. She was extremely handsome, and was considered a model as wife and mother. Catalani was very fond of money, and would never sing unless paid beforehand. She was invited, with her husband, to pass some time at Stowe, where a numerous but select party had been invited; and Madame Catalani, being asked to sing soon after dinner, willingly complied. When the day of her departure came, her husband placed in the hands of the Marquis of Buckingham the following little billet:--"For seventeen songs, seventeen hundred pounds." This large sum was paid at once, without hesitation; proving that Lord Buckingham was a refined gentleman, in every sense of the word.

Catalani's husband, M. de Valabreque, once fought a duel with a German baron who had insulted the prima donna; the weapons used were sabres, and Valabreque cut half of the Baron's nose clean off. Madame Catalani lived for many years, highly respected, at a handsome villa near Florence. Her two sons are now distinguished members of the Imperial court in Paris; the eldest being Prefet du Palais, and the youngest colonel of a regiment of hussars.

When George the Fourth was Regent, Her Majesty's Theatre, as the Italian Opera in the Haymarket is still called, was conducted on a very different system from that which now prevails. Some years previous to the period to which I refer, no one could obtain a box or a ticket for the pit without a voucher from one of the lady patronesses; who, in 1805, were the Duchesses of Marlborough, Devonshire, and Bedford, Lady Carlisle, and some others. In their day, after, the singing and the ballet were over, the company used to retire into the concert-room, where a ball took place, accompanied by refreshments and a supper. There all the rank and fashion of England were assembled on a sort of neutral ground. At a later period, the management of the Opera House fell into the hands of Mr. Waters, when it became less difficult to obtain admittance; but the strictest etiquette was still kept up as regarded the dress of the gentlemen, who were only admitted with knee-buckles, ruffles, and chapeau bras. If there happened to be a drawing-room, the ladies would appear in their court-dresses, as well as the gentlemen, and on all occasions the audience of Her Majesty's Theatre was stamped with aristocratic elegance. In the boxes of the first tier might have been seen the daughters of the Duchess of Argyle, four of England's beauties; in the next box were the equally lovely Marchioness of Stafford and her daughter, Lady Elizabeth Gore, now the Duchess of Norfolk: not less remarkable was Lady Harrowby and her daughters Lady Susan and Lady Mary Ryder. The peculiar type of female beauty which these ladies so attractively exemplified, is such as can be met with only in the British Isles: the full, round, soul-inspired eye of Italy, and the dark hair of the sunny south, often combined with that exquisitely pearly complexion which seems to be concomitant with humidity and fog. You could scarcely gaze upon the peculiar beauty to which I refer without being as much charmed with its kindly expression as with its physical loveliness.

DINING AND COOKERY IN ENGLAND FIFTY YEARS AGO

England can boast of a Spenser, Shakspeare, Milton, and many other illustrious poets, clearly indicating that the national character of Britons is not deficient in imagination; but we have not had one single masculine inventive genius of the kitchen. It is the probable result of our national antipathy to mysterious culinary compounds, that none of the bright minds of England have ventured into the region of scientific cookery. Even in the best houses, when I was a young man, the dinners were wonderfully solid, hot and stimulating. The menu of a grand dinner was thus composed:--Mulligatawny and turtle soups were the first dishes placed before you; a little lower, the eye met with the familiar salmon at one end of the table, and the turbot, surrounded by smelts, at the other. The first course was sure to be followed by a saddle of mutton or a piece of roast beef; and then you could take your oath that fowls, tongue, and ham, would as assuredly succeed as darkness after day.

Whilst these never ending pieces de resistance were occupying the table, what were called French dishes were, for custom's sake, added to the solid abundance. The French, or side dishes, consisted of very mild but very abortive attempts at Continental cooking, and I have always observed that they met with the neglect and contempt that they merited. The universally adored and ever popular boiled potato, produced at the very earliest period of the dinner, was eaten with every-thing, up to the moment when sweets appeared. Our vegetables, the best in the world, were never honoured by an accompanying sauce, and generally came to the table cold. A prime difficulty to overcome was the placing on your fork, and finally in your mouth, some half-dozen different eatables which occupied your plate at the same time. For example, your plate would contain, say, a slice of turkey, a piece of stuffing, a sausage, pickles, a slice of tongue, cauliflower, and potatoes. Accord-ing to habit and custom, a judicious and careful selection from this little bazaar of good things was to be made, with an endeavour to place a portion of each in your mouth at the same moment. In fact, it appeared to me that we used to do all our compound cookery between our jaws. The dessert--generally ordered at Messrs. Grange's, or at Owen's, in Bond Street--if for a dozen people, would cost at least as many pounds. The wines were chiefly port, sherry, and hock; claret, and even Bur-gundy, being then designated "poor, thin, washy stuff." A perpetual thirst seemed to come over people, both men and women, as soon as they had tasted their soup; as from that moment everybody was taking wine with everybody else till the close of the dinner; and such wine as produced that class of cordiality which frequently wanders into stupefaction. How all this sort of eating and drinking ended was obvi-ous, from the prevalence of gout, and the necessity of everyone making the pill-box their constant bedroom companion.

THE PRINCE REGENT

When the eldest son of George the Third assumed the Regency, England was in a state of political transition. The convulsions of the Continent were felt amongst us; the very foundations of European society were shaking, and the social relations of men were rapidly changing. The Regent's natural leanings were towards the Tories; therefore as soon as he undertook the responsibility of power, he abruptly abandoned the Whigs and retained in office the admirers and partisans of his father's policy. This resolution caused him to have innumerable and inveterate enemies, who never lost an opportunity of attacking his public acts and interfering with his domestic relations.

The Regent was singularly imbued with petty royal pride. He would rather be amiable and familiar with his tailor than agreeable and friendly with the most illustrious of the aristocracy of Great Britain; he would rather joke with a Brummell than admit to his confidence a Norfolk or a Somerset. The Regent was always particularly well-bred in public, and showed, if he chose, decidedly good manners; but he was in the habit very often of addressing himself in preference to those whom he felt he could patronise. His Royal Highness was as much the victim of circumstances and the child of thoughtless imprudence as the most humble subject of the crown. His unfortunate marriage with a Princess of Brunswick originated in his debts; as he married that unhappy lady for one million sterling, William Pitt being the contractor! The Princess of Wales married nothing but an association with the Crown of England. If the Prince ever seriously loved any woman, it was Mrs. Fitzherbert, with whom he had appeared at the altar.

Public opinion in England, under the inspiration of the Whigs, raised a cry of indignation against the Prince. It was imagined, I presume, that royal personage should be born without heart or feeling; that he should have been able to live only for the good of the State and for the convenience of his creditors. The Princess of Wales was one of the most unattractive and almost repulsive women for an elegant-minded man that could well have been found amongst German royalty. It is not my intention to recall the events of the Regency. It is well known that the Prince became eventually so unpopular as to exclude himself as much as possible from public gaze. His intimate companions, after the trial of Queen Caroline, were Lords Cunningham and Fife, Sir Benjamin Bloomfield, Sir William Macmahon, Admiral Nagle, Sir A. Barnard, Lords Glenlyon, Hertford, and Lowther. These gentlemen generally dined with him; the dinner being the artistic product of that famous gastronomic savant, Wattiers. The Prince was very fond of listening after dinner to the gossip of society. When he became George the Fourth, no change took place in these personnels at the banquet, excepting that with the fruits and flowers of the table was introduced the beautiful Marchioness of Conyngham, whose brilliant wit, according to the estimation of his Majesty, surpassed that of any other of his friends, male or female.

PRINCESS CHARLOTTE OF WALES AT A FETE IN THE YEAR 1813, AT CARLTON HOUSE

Carlton House, at the period to which I refer, was a centre for all the great politicians and wits who were the favorites of the Regent. The principal entrance of this palace in Pall Mall, with its screen of columns, will be remembered by many. In the rear of the mansion was an extensive garden that reached from Warwick Street to Marlborough House; green sward, stately trees, (probably two hundred years old), and beds of the choicest flowers, gave to the grounds a picturesque attraction perhaps unequalled. It was here that the heir to the throne of England gave, in 1813, an open-air fete, in honour of the battle of Vittoria. About three o'clock P.M. the elite of London society, who had been honoured with an invitation, began to arrive--all in full dress; the ladies particularly displaying their diamonds and pearls, as if they were going to a drawing-room. The men were, of course, in full dress, wearing knee-buckles. The regal circle was composed of the Queen, the Regent, the Princess Sophia and Mary, the Princess Charlotte, the Dukes of York, Clarence, Cumberland, and Cambridge.

This was the first day that her Royal Highness the Princess Charlotte appeared in public. She was a young lady of more than ordinary personal attractions; her features were regular, and her complexion fair, with the rich bloom of youthful beauty; her eyes were blue and very expressive, and her hair was abundant, and of that peculiar light brown which merges into the golden: in fact, such hair as the Middle-Age Italian painters associate with their conceptions of the Madonna. In figure her Royal Highness was somewhat over the ordinary height of women, but finely proportioned and well developed. Her manners were remarkable for a simplicity and good-nature which would have won admiration and invited affection in the most humble walks of life. She created universal admiration, and I may say a feeling of national pride, amongst all who attended the ball. The Prince Regent entered the gardens giving his arm to the Queen, the rest of the royal family following. Tents had been erected in various parts of the grounds, where the bands of the Guards were stationed. The weather was magnificent, a circumstance which contributed to show off the admirable arrangements of Sir Benjamin Bloomfield, to whom had been deputed the organization of the fete, which commenced by dancing on the lawn.

The Princess Charlotte honoured with her presence two dances. In the first she accepted the hand of the late Duke of Devonshire, and in the second that of the Earl of Aboyne, who had danced with Marie Antoinette, and who, as Lord Huntley, lived long enough to dance with Queen Victoria. The Princess entered so much into the spirit of the fete as to ask for the then fashionable Scotch dances. The Prince was dressed in the Windsor uniform, and wore the garter and star. He made himself very amiable, and conversed much with the Ladies Hertford, Cholmondeley, and Montford. Altogether, the fete was a memorable event.

A year afterwards, the Duke of York said to his royal niece, "Tell me, my dear, have you seen anyone among the foreign princes whom you would like to have for a husband?" The Princess naively replied, "No one so much prepossesses me as Prince Leopold of Coburg. I have heard much of his bravery in the field, and I must say he is personally agreeable to me. I have particularly heard of his famous cavalry charge at the battle of Leipsic, where he took several thousand prisoners, for which he was rewarded with the Order of Maria Therese." In a few months afterwards she became the wife of the man whom she so much admired, and from whom she was torn away not long after by the cruel hand of death. It will be remembered that she died in childbirth, and her offspring expired at the same time. The accoucheur who attended her was so much affected by the calamity, that he committed suicide some short time afterwards.

BEAU BRUMMELL

Amongst the curious freaks of fortune there is none more remarkable in my memory than the sudden appearance, in the highest and best society in London, of a young man whose antecedents warranted a much less conspicuous career: I refer to the famous Beau Brummell. We have innumerable instances of soldiers, lawyers, and men of letters, elevating themselves from the most humble stations, and becoming the companions of princes and lawgivers; but there are comparatively few examples of men obtaining a similarly elevated position simply from their attractive personal appearance and fascinating manners. Brummell's father, who was a steward to one or two large estates, sent his son George to Eton. He was endowed with a handsome person, and distinguished himself at Eton as the best scholar, the best boatman, and the best cricketer; and, more than all, he was supposed to possess the comprehensive excellences that are represented by the familiar term of "good fellow." He made many friends amongst the scions of good families, by whom he was considered a sort of Crichton; and his reputation reached a circle over which reigned the celebrated Duchess of Devonshire. At a grand ball given by her Grace, George Brummell, then quite a youth, appeared for the first time in such elevated society. He immediately became a great favourite with the ladies, and was asked by all the dowagers to as many balls and soirees as he could attend.

At last the Prince of Wales sent for Brummell, and was so much pleased with his manner and appearance, that he gave him a commission in his own regiment, the 10th Hussars. Unluckily, Brummell, soon after joining his regiment, was thrown from his horse at a grand review at Brighton, when he broke his classical Roman nose. This misfortune, however, did not affect the fame of the beau; and although his nasal organ had undergone a slight transformation, it was forgiven by his admirers, since the rest of his person remained intact. When we are prepossessed by the attractions of a favourite, it is not a trifle that will dispel the illusion; and Brummell continued to govern society, in conjunction with the Prince of Wales. He was remarkable for his dress, which was generally conceived by himself; the execution of his sublime imagination being carried out by that superior genius, Mr. Weston, tailor, of Old Bond Street. The Regent sympathised deeply with Brummell's labours to arrive at the most attractive and gentlemanly mode of dressing the male form, at a period when fashion had placed at the disposal of the tailor the most hideous material that could possibly tax his art. The coat may have a long tail or a short tail, a high collar or a low collar, but it will always be an ugly garment. The modern hat may be spread out at the top, or narrowed, whilst the brim may be turned up or turned down, made a little wider or a little more narrow, still it is inconceivably hideous. Pantaloons and Hessian boots were the least objectionable features of the costume which the imagination of a Brummell and the genius of a Royal Prince were called upon to modify or change. The hours of meditative agony which each dedicated to the odious fashions of the day have left no monument save the coloured caricatures in which these illustrious persons have appeared.

Brummell, at this time, besides being the companion and friend of the Prince, was very intimate with the Dukes of Rutland, Dorset, and Argyll, Lords Sefton, Alvanley, and Plymouth. In the zenith of his popularity he might be seen at the bay window of White's Club, surrounded by the lions of the day, laying down the law, and occasionally indulging in those witty remarks for which he was famous. His house in Chapel Street corresponded with his personal "get up"; the furniture was in excellent taste, and the library contained the best works of the best authors of every period and of every country. His canes, his snuff-boxes, his Sevres china, were exquisite; his horses and carriage were conspicuous for their excellence; and, in fact, the superior taste of a Brummell was discoverable in everything that belonged to him.

But the reign of the king of fashion, like all other reigns, was not destined to continue for ever. Brummell warmly espoused the cause of Mrs. Fitzherbert, and this of course offended the Prince of Wales. I refer to the period when his Royal Highness had abandoned that beautiful woman for another favourite. A coldness sprang up between the Prince and his protege, and finally, the mirror of fashion was excluded from the royal presence. A curious accident brought Brummell again to the dinner-table of his royal patron; he was asked one night at White's to take a hand at whist, when he won from George Harley Drummond 20,000L. This circumstance having been related by the Duke of York to the Prince of Wales, the beau was again invited to Carlton House. At the commencement of the dinner, matters went off smoothly; but Brummell, in his joy at finding himself with his old friend, became excited, and drank too much wine. His Royal Highness--who wanted to pay off Brummell for an insult he had received at Lady Cholmondeley's ball, when the beau, turning towards the Prince, said to Lady Worcester, "Who is your fat friend?"--had invited him to dinner merely out of a desire for revenge. The Prince therefore pretended to be affronted with Brummell's hilarity, and said to his brother, the Duke of York, who was present, "I think we had better order Mr. Brummell's carriage before he gets drunk." Whereupon he rang the bell, and Brummell left the royal presence. This circumstance originated the story about the beau having told the Prince to ring the bell. I received these details from the late General Sir Arthur Upton, who was present at the dinner. The latter days of Brummell were clouded with mortifications and penury. He retired to Calais, where he kept up a ludicrous imitation of his past habits. At least he got himself named consul at Caen; but he afterwards lost the appointment, and eventually died insane, and in abject poverty, either at Boulogne or Calais.

ROMEO COATES

This singular man, more than forty years ago, occupied a large portion of public attention; his eccentricities were the theme of general wonder, and great was the curiosity to catch a glance at as strange a being as any that ever appeared in English society. This extraordinary individual was a native of one of the West India Islands, and was represented as a man of extraordinary wealth; to which, however, he had no claim.

About the year 1808 there arrived at the York Hotel, at Bath, a person about the age of fifty, somewhat gentlemanlike, but so different from the usual men of the day that considerable attention was directed to him. He was of a good figure; but his face was sallow, seamed with wrinkles, and more expressive of cunning than of any other quality. His dress was remarkable: in the day-time he was covered at all seasons with enormous quantities of fur; but the evening costume in which he went to the balls made a great impression, from its gaudy appearance; for his buttons as well as his knee-buckles were of diamonds. There was of course great curiosity to know who this stranger was; and this curiosity was heightened by an announcement that he proposed to appear at the theatre in the character of Romeo. There was something so unlike the impassioned lover in his appearance--so much that indicated a man with few intellectual gifts--that everybody was prepared for a failure. No one, however, anticipated the reality.

On the night fixed for his appearance the house was crowded to suffocation. The playbills had given out that "an amateur of fashion" would for that night only perform in the character of Romeo; besides, it was generally whispered that the rehearsals gave indication of comedy rather than tragedy, and that his readings were of a perfectly novel character.

The very first appearance of Romeo convulsed the house with laughter. Benvolio prepares the audience for the stealthy visit of the lover to the object of his admiration; and fully did the amateur give the expression to one sense of the words uttered, for he was indeed the true representative of a thief stealing onwards in the night, "with Tarquin's ravishing strides," and disguising his face as if he were thoroughly ashamed of it. The darkness of the scene did not, however, show his real character so much as the masquerade, when he came forward with hideous grin, and made what he considered his bow,--which consisted in thrusting his head forward and bobbing it up and down several times, his body remaining perfectly upright and stiff, like a toy mandarin with moveable head.

His dress was outre in the extreme: whether Spanish, Italian, or English, no one could say; it was like nothing ever worn. In a cloak of sky-blue silk, profusely spangled, red pantaloons, a vest of white muslin, surmounted by an enormously thick cravat, and a wig a la Charles the Second, capped by an opera hat, he presented one of the most grotesque spectacles ever witnessed upon the stage. The whole of his garments were evidently too tight for him; and his movements appeared so incongruous, that every time he raised his arm, or moved a limb, it was impossible to refrain from laughter: but what chiefly convulsed the audience was the bursting of a seam in an inexpressible part of his dress, and the sudden extrusion through the red rent of a quantity of white linen sufficient to make a Bourbon flag, which was visible whenever he turned round. This was at first supposed to be a wilful offence against common decency, and some disapprobation was evinced; but the utter unconsciousness of the odd creature was soon apparent, and then urestrained mirth reigned throughout the boxes, pit, and gallery. The total want of flexibility of limb, the awkwardness of his gait, and the idiotic manner in which he stood still, all produced a most ludicrous effect; but when his guttural voice was heard, and his total misapprehension of every passage in the play, especially the vulgarity of his address to Juliet, were perceived, everyone was satisfied that Shakspeare's Romeo was burlesqued on that occasion.

The balcony scene was interrupted by shrieks of laughter, for in the midst of one of Juliet's impassioned exclamations, Romeo quietly took out his snuff-box and applied a pinch to his nose; on this a wag in the gallery bawled out, "I say, Romeo, give us a pinch," when the impassioned lover, in the most affected manner, walked to the side boxes and offered the contents of his box first to the gentlemen, and then, with great gallantry, to the ladies. This new interpretation of Shakspeare was hailed with loud bravos, which the actor acknowledged with his usual grin and nod. Romeo then returned to the balcony, and was seen to extend his arms; but all passed in dumb show, so incessant were the shouts of laughter. All that went on upon the stage was for a time quite inaudible, but previous to the soliloquy "I do remember an apothecary," there was for a moment a dead silence; for in rushed the hero with a precipitate step until he reached the stage lamps, when he commenced his speech in the lowest possible whisper, as if he had something to communicate to the pit that ought not to be generally known; and this tone was kept up throughout the whole of the soliloquy, so that not a sound could be heard.

The amateur actor showed many indications of aberration of mind, and seemed rather the object of pity than of amusement; he, however, appeared delighted with himself, and also with his audience, for at the conclusion he walked first to the left of the stage and bobbed his head in his usual grotesque manner at the side boxes; then to the right, performing the same feat; after which, going to the centre of the stage with the usual bob, and placing his hand upon his left breast, he exclaimed, "Haven't I done it well?" To this inquiry the house, convulsed as it was with shouts of laughter, responded in such a way as delighted the heart of Kean on one great occasion, when he said, "The pit rose at me." The whole audience started up as if with one accord, giving a yell of derision, whilst pocket-handkerchiefs waved from all parts of the theatre.

The dying scene was irresistibly comic, and I question if Liston, Munden, or Joey Knight, was ever greeted with such merriment; for Romeo dragged the unfortunate Juliet from the tomb, much in the same manner as a washerwoman thrusts into her cart the bag of foul linen. But how shall I describe his death? Out came a dirty silk handkerchief from his pocket, with which he carefully swept the ground; then his opera hat was carefully placed for a pillow, and down he laid himself. After various tossings about he seemed reconciled to the position; but the house vociferously bawled out, "Die again, Romeo!" and, obedient to the command, he rose up, and went through the ceremony again. Scarcely had he lain quietly down, when the call was again heard, and the well-pleased amateur was evidently prepared to enact a third death; but Juliet now rose up from her tomb, and gracefully put an end to this ludicrous scene by advancing to the front of the stage and aptly applying a quotation from Shakspeare:--

"Dying is such sweet sorrow,
That he will die again until to-morrow."

Thus ended an extravaganza such as has seldom been witnessed; for although Coates repeated the play at the Haymarket, amidst shouts of laughter from the playgoers, there never was so ludicrous a performance as that which took place at Bath on the first night of his appearance. Eventually he was driven from the stage with much contumely, in consequence of its having been discovered that, under pretence of acting for a charitable purpose, he had obtained a sum of money for his performances. His love of notoriety led him to have a most singular shell-shaped carriage built, in which, drawn by two fine white horses, he was wont to parade in the park; the harness, and every available part of the vehicle (which was really handsome) were blazoned over with his heraldic device--a cock crowing, and his appearance was heralded by the gamins of London shrieking out "cock-a-doodle-doo." Coates eventually quitted London and settled at Boulogne, where a fair lady was induced to become the partner of his existence, notwithstanding the ridicule of the whole world.

HYDE PARK AFTER THE PENINSULAR WAR

That extensive district of park land, the entrances of which are in Piccadilly and Oxford Street, was far more rural in appearance in 1815 than at the present day. Under the trees cows and deer were grazing; the paths were fewer and none told of that perpetual tread of human feet which now destroys all idea of country charms and illusions. As you gazed from an eminence, no rows of monotonous houses reminded you of the vicinity of a large city, and the atmosphere of Hyde Park was then much more like what God has made it than the hazy, gray, coal-darkened half-twilight of the London of to-day. The company which then congregated daily about five, was composed of dandies and women in the best society; the men mounted on such horses as England alone could then produce. The dandy's dress consisted of a blue coat with brass buttons, leather breeches, and top boots; and it was the fashion to wear a deep, stiff white cravat, which prevented you from seeing your boots while standing. All the world watched Brummell to imitate him, and order their clothes of the tradesman who dressed that sublime dandy. One day a youthful beau approached Brummell and said, "Permit me to ask you where you get your blacking?" "Ah!" replied Brummell, gazing complacently at his boots, "my blacking positively ruins me. I will tell you in confidence; it is made with the finest champagne!"

Many of the ladies used to drive into the park in a carriage called a vis-a-vis, which held only two persons. The hammer-cloth, rich in heraldic designs, the powdered footmen in smart liveries, and a coachman who assumed all the gaiety and appearance of a wigged archbishop, were indispensable. The equipages were generally much more gorgeous than at a later period, when democracy invaded the parks, and introduced what may be termed a "brummagem society," with shabby-genteel carriages and servants. The carriage company consisted of the most celebrated beauties, amongst whom were remarked the Duchesses of Rutland, Argyle, Gordon, and Bedford, Ladies Cowper, Foley, Heathcote, Louisa Lambton, Hertford, and Mountjoy. The most conspicuous horsemen were the Prince Regent (accompanied by Sir Benjamin Bloomfield); the Duke of York and his old friend, Warwick Lake; the Duke of Dorset, on his white horse; the Marquis of Anglesea, with his lovely daughters; Lord Harrowby and the Ladies Ryder; the Earl of Sefton and the Ladies Molyneux; and the eccentric Earl of Moreton on his long-tailed grey. In those days "pretty horsebreakers" would not have dared to show themselves in Hyde Park; nor did you see any of the lower or middle classes of London intruding themselves in regions which, with a sort of tacit understanding, were then given up exclusively to persons of rank and fashion.

LONDON HOTELS IN 1814

There was a class of men, of very high rank, such as Lords Wellington, Nelson, and Collingwood, Sir John Moore and some few others who never frequented the clubs. The persons to whom I refer, and amongst whom were many members of the sporting world, used to congregate at a few hotels. The Clarendon, Limmer's, Ibbetson's, Fladong's, Stephens', and Grillon's, were the fashionable hotels. The Clarendon was then kept by a French cook, Jacquiers, who contrived to amass a large sum of money in the service of Louis the Eighteenth in England, and subsequently with Lord Darnley. This was the only public hotel where you could get a genuine French dinner, and for which you seldom paid less than three or four pounds; your bottle of champagne or of claret, in the year 1814, costing you a guinea.

Limmer's was an evening resort for the sporting world; in fact, it was a midnight Tattersal's, where you heard nothing but the language of the turf, and where men with not very clean hands used to make up their books. Limmer's was the most dirty hotel in London; but in the gloomy, comfortless coffee-room might be seen many members of the rich squirearchy, who visited London during the sporting season. This hotel was frequently so crowded that a bed could not be obtained for any amount of money; but you could always get a very good plain English dinner, an excellent bottle of port, and some famous gin-punch. Ibbetson's hotel was chiefly patronized by the clergy and young men from the universities. The charges there were more economical than at similar establishments. Fladong's, in Oxford Street, was chiefly frequented by naval men; for in those days there was no club for sailors. Stephens', in Bond Street, was a fashionable hotel, supported by officers of the army and men about town. If a stranger asked to dine there, he was stared at by the servants, and very solemnly assured that there was no table vacant. It was not an uncommon thing to see thirty or forty saddle-horses and tilburys waiting outside this hotel. I recollect two of my old Welsh friends, who used each of them to dispose of five bottles of wine daily, residing here in 1815, when the familiar joints, boiled fish and fried soles, were the only eatables you could order.

THE CLUBS OF LONDON IN 1814

The members of the clubs in London, many years since, were persons, almost without exception, belonging exclusively to the aristocratic world. "My trades-men," as King Allen used to call the bankers and the merchants, had not then invaded White's, Boodle's, Brookes', or Wattiers', in Bolton Street, Piccadilly; which, with the Guards, Arthur's, and Graham's, were the only clubs at the West End of the town. White's was decidedly the most difficult of entry; its list of members comprised nearly all the noble names of Great Britain.

The politics of White's club were then decidedly Tory. It was here that play was carried on to an extent which made many ravages in large fortunes, the traces of which have not disappeared at the present day. General Scott, the father-in-law of George Canning and the Duke of Portland, was known to have won at White's 200,000L.; thanks to his notorious sobriety and knowledge of the game of whist. The General possessed a great advantage over his companions by avoiding those indulgences at the table which used to muddle other men's brains. He confined himself to dining off something like a boiled chicken, with toast-and-water; by such a regimen he came to the whist-table with a clear head, and possessing as he did a remarkable memory, with great coolness and judgment, he was able honestly to win the enormous sum of 200,000L. At Brookes', for nearly half a century, the play was of a more gambling character than at White's. Faro and macao were indulged in to an extent which enabled a man to win or to lose a considerable fortune in one night. It was here that Charles James Fox, Selwyn, Lord Carlisle, Lord Robert Spencer, General Fitzpatrick, and other great Whigs, won and lost hundreds of thousands; frequently remaining at the table for many hours without rising.

On one occasion, Lord Robert Spencer contrived to lose the last shilling of his considerable fortune, given him by his brother, the Duke of Marlborough; General Fitzpatrick being much in the same condition, they agreed to raise a sum of money, in order that they might keep a faro bank. The members of the club made no objection, and ere long they carried out their design. As is generally the case, the bank was a winner, and Lord Robert bagged, as his share of the proceeds, 100,000L. He retired, strange to say, from the foetid atmosphere of play, with the money in his pocket, and never again gambled. George Harley Drummond, of the famous banking-house, Charing Cross, only played once in his whole life at White's Club at whist, on which occasion he lost 20,000L. to Brummell. This event caused him to retire from the banking-house of which he was a partner.

Lord Carlisle was one of the most remarkable victims amongst the players at Brookes', and Charles Fox, his friend, was not more fortunate, being subsequently always in pecuniary difficulties. Many a time, after a long night of hard play, the loser found himself at the Israelitish establishment of Howard and Gibbs, then the fashionable and patronized money-lenders. These gentlemen never failed to make hard terms with the borrower, although ample security was invariably demanded.

The Guards' Club was established for the three regiments of Foot Guards, and was conducted upon a military system. Billiards and low whist were the only games indulged in. The dinner was, perhaps, better than at most clubs, and considerably cheaper. I had the honour of being a member for several years, during which time I have nothing to remember but the most agreeable incidents. Arthur's and Graham's were less aristocratic than those I have mentioned; it was at the latter, thirty years ago, that a most painful circumstance took place. A nobleman of the highest position and influence in society was detected in cheating at cards, and after a trial, which did not terminate in his favour, he died of a broken heart.

Upon one occasion, some gentlemen of both White's and Brookes' had the honour to dine with the Prince Regent, and during the conversation, the Prince inquired what sort of dinners they got at their clubs; upon which, Sir Thomas Stepney, one of the guests, observed that their dinners were always the same, "the eternal joints, or beefsteaks, the boiled fowl with oyster sauce, and an apple tart--this is what we have, sir, at our clubs, and very monotonous fare it is." The Prince, without further remark, rang the bell for his cook, Wattier, and, in the presence of those who dined at the Royal table, asked him whether he would take a house and organize a dinner club. Wattier assented, and named Madison, the Prince's page, manager, and Labourie, the cook, from the Royal kitchen. The club flourished only a few years, owing to the high play that was carried on there. The Duke of York patronized it, and was a member. I was a member in 1816, and frequently saw his Royal Highness there. The dinners were exquisite; the best Parisian cooks could not beat Labourie. The favourite game played there was macao. Upon one occasion, Jack Bouvrie, brother of Lady Heytesbury, was losing large sums, and became very irritable; Raikes, with bad taste, laughed at Bouverie, and attempted to amuse us with some of his stale jokes; upon which, Bouverie threw his play-bowl, with the few counters it contained, at Raikes's head; unfortunately it struck him, and made the City dandy angry, but no serious results followed this open insult.

REMARKABLE CHARACTERS OF LONDON ABOUT THE YEARS 1814, 1815, 1816

It appears to be a law of natural history that every generation produces and throws out from the mob of society a few conspicuous men, that pass under the general appellation of "men about town." Michael Angelo Taylor was one of those remarkable individuals whom everyone was glad to know; and those who had not that privilege were ever talking about him, although he was considered by many a bit of a bore. Michael Angelo was a Member of Parliament for many years, and generally sat in one of the most important committees of the House of Commons; for he was a man of authority and an attractive speaker. In appearance he was one of that sort of persons whom you could not pass in the streets without exclaiming, "Who can that be?" His face blushed with port wine, the purple tints of which, by contrast, caused his white hair to glitter with silvery brightness; he wore leather breeches, top boots, blue coat, white waistcoat, and an unstarched and exquisitely white neckcloth, the whole surmounted by a very broad-brimmed beaver;--such was the dress of the universally known Michael Angelo Taylor. If you met him in society, or at the clubs, he was never known to salute you but with the invariable phrase, "What news have you?" Upon one occasion, riding through St. James's Park, he met the great Minister, Mr. Pitt, coming from Wimbledon, where he resided. He asked Mr. Pitt the usual question, upon which the Premier replied, "I have not yet seen the morning papers."

"Oh, that won't do, Mr. Pitt. I am Sure that you know something, and will not tell me." Mr. Pitt good-humouredly replied: "Well, then, I am going to a Cabinet Council, and I will consult my colleagues whether I can divulge State secrets to you or not." Upon another occasion, on entering Boodle's, of which he was a member, he observed the celebrated Lord Westmoreland at table, where the noble lord was doing justice to a roast fowl. Taylor, of course, asked him the news of the day, and Lord Westmoreland coolly told the little newsmonger to go into the other room and leave him to finish his dinner, promising to join him after he had done. The noble Lord kept his word, and the first thing he heard from Mr. Taylor was, "Well, my lord, what news? what had you for dinner?"

His lordship replied, "A Welsh leg of mutton." "What then--what then?" "Don't you think a leg of mutton enough for any man?" "Yes, my lord, but you did not eat it all." "Yes, Taylor, I did." "Well, I think you have placed the leg of mutton in some mysterious place, for I see no trace of it in your lean person."

Lord Westmoreland was remarkable for an appetite which made nothing of a respectable joint, or a couple of fowls.

I know not whether Mr. Poole, the author of Paul Pry, had Michael Angelo in his head when he wrote that well-known comedy; but certainly he might have sat for a character whose intrusive and inquisitive habits were so notorious, that people on seeing him approach always prepared for a string of almost impertinent interrogations.

Another remarkable man about town was Colonel Cooke, commonly called Kangaroo Cooke, who was for many years the private aide-de-camp and secretary of H. R. H. the Duke of York. He was the brother of General Sir George Cooke and of the beautiful Countess of Cardigan, mother of the gallant Lord Cardigan, and the Ladies Howe, Baring, and Lucan. During his career he had been employed in diplomatic negotiations with the French, previous to the peace of Paris. He was in the best society, and always attracted attention by his dandified mode of dress.

Colonel Armstrong, another pet of the Duke of York, was known, when in the Coldstream Guards, to be a thorough hard-working soldier, and his non-commissioned officers were so perfect, that nearly all the adjutants of the different regiments of the line were educated by him. He was a strict disciplinarian, but strongly opposed to corporal punishment, and used to boast that during the whole time that he commanded the regiment only two men had been flogged.

Colonel Mackinnon, commonly called "Dan," was an exceedingly well-made man, and remarkable for his physical powers in running, jumping, climbing, and such bodily exercises as demanded agility and muscular strength. He used to amuse his friends by creeping over the furniture of a room like a monkey. It was very common for his companions to make bets with him: for example, that he would not be able to climb up the ceiling of a room, or scramble over a certain house-top. Grimaldi, the famous clown, used to say, "Colonel Mackinnon has only to put on the motley costume, and he would totally eclipse me."

Mackinnon was famous for practical jokes; which were, however, always played in a gentlemanly way. Before landing at St. Andero's, with some other officers who had been on leave in England, he agreed to personate the Duke of York, and make the Spaniards believe that his Royal Highness was amongst them. On nearing the shore, a royal standard was hoisted at the masthead, and Mackinnon disembarked, wearing the star of his shako on his left breast, and accompanied by his friends, who agreed to play the part of aides-de-camp to royalty. The Spanish authorities were soon informed of the arrival of the Royal Commander-in-Chief of the British army; so they received Mackinnon with the usual pomp and circumstance attending such occasions. The mayor of the place, in honour of the illustrious arrival, gave a grand banquet, which terminated with the appearance of a huge bowl of punch. Whereupon Dan, thinking that the joke had gone far enough, suddenly dived his head into the porcelain vase, and threw his heels into the air. The surprise and indignation of the solemn Spaniards was such, that they made a most intemperate report of the hoax that had been played on them to Lord Wellington; Dan, however, was ultimately forgiven, after a severe reprimand.

Another of his freaks very nearly brought him to a court-martial. Lord Wellington was curious about visiting a convent near Lisbon, and the lady abbess made no difficulty; Mackinnon, hearing this, contrived to get clandestinely within the sacred walls, and it was generally supposed that it was neither his first nor his second visit. At all events, when Lord Wellington arrived, Dan Mackinnon was to be seen among the nuns, dressed out in their sacred costume, with his head and whiskers shaved, and as he possessed good features, he was declared to be one of the best-looking amongst those chaste dames. It was supposed that this adventure, which was known to Lord Byron, suggested a similar episode in Don Juan, the scene being laid in the East. I might say more about Dan's adventures in the convent, but have no wish to be scandalous.

Another dandy of the day was Sir Lumley Skeffington, who used to paint his face, so that he looked like a French toy; he dressed a la Robespierre, and practised other follies, although the consummate old fop was a man of literary attainments, and a great admirer and patron of the drama. Skeffington was remarkable for his politeness and courtly manners; in fact, he was invited everywhere, and was very popular with the ladies. You always knew of his approach by an avant-courier of sweet smells; and when he advanced a little nearer, you might suppose yourself in the atmosphere of a perfumer's shop. He is thus immortalized by Byron, in the English Bards and Scotch Reviewers, alluding to the play written by Skeffington, The Sleeping Beauty:--

"In grim array though Lewis' spectres rise,
Still Skeffington and Goose divide the prize:
And sure great Skeffington must claim our praise,
For skirtless coats and skeletons of plays
Renowned alike; whose genius ne'er confines
Her flight to garnish Greenwood's gay designs,
Nor sleeps with 'sleeping beauties' but anon
In five facetious acts comes thundering on,
While poor John Bull, bewildered with the scene,
Stares, wondering what the devil it can mean;
But as some hands applaud--a venal few--
Rather than sleep, John Bull applauds it too."

Long Wellesley Pole was a fashionable who distinguished himself by giving sumptuous dinners at Wanstead, where he owned one of the finest mansions in England. He used to ask his friends to dine with him after the opera at midnight;

the drive from London being considered appetisant. Every luxury that money could command was placed before his guests at this unusual hour of the night. He married Miss Tylney Pole, an heiress of fifty thousand a-year, yet died quite a beggar: in fact, he would have starved, had it not been for the charity of his cousin, the present Duke of Wellington, who allowed him three hundred a-year.

THE GUARDS MARCHING FROM ENGHIEN ON THE 15TH OF JUNE

Two battalions of my regiment had started from Brussels; the other (the 2nd), to which I belonged, remained in London, and I saw no prospect of taking part in the great events which were about to take place on the Continent. Early in June I had the honour of dining with Colonel Darling, the deputy adjutant-general, and I was there introduced to Sir Thomas Picton, as a countryman and neighbour of his brother, Mr. Turbeville, of Evenney Abbey, in Glamorganshire. He was very gracious, and, on his two aides-de-camp--Major Tyler and my friend Chambers, of the Guards--lamenting that I was obliged to remain at home, Sir Thomas said, "Is the lad really anxious to go out?" Chambers answered that it was the height of my ambition. Sir Thomas inquired if all the appointments to his staff were filled up; and then added, with a grim smile, "If Tyler is killed, which is not at all unlikely, I do not know why I should not take my young countryman: he may go over with me if he can get leave." I was overjoyed at this, and, after thanking the General a thousand times, made my bow and retired.

I was much elated at the thoughts of being Picton's aide-de-camp, though that somewhat remote contingency depended upon my friends Tyler, or Chambers, or others, meeting with an untimely end; but at eighteen on ne doute de rien. So I set about thinking how I should manage to get my outfit, in order to appear at Brussels in a manner worthy of the aide-de-camp of the great General. As my funds were at a low ebb, I went to Cox and Greenwood's, those staunch friends of the hard-up soldier. Sailors may talk of the "little cherub that sits up aloft," but commend me for liberality, kindness, and generosity, to my old friends in Craig's Court. I there obtained 200L., which I took with me to a gambling-house in St. James' Square, where I managed, by some wonderful accident, to win 600L.; and, having thus obtained the sinews of war, I made numerous purchases, amongst others two first-rate horses at Tattersall's for a high figure, which were embarked for Ostend, along with my groom. I had not got leave; but I thought I should get back, after the great battle that appeared imminent, in time to mount guard at St. James's. On a Saturday I accompanied Chambers in his carriage to Ramsgate, where Sir Thomas Picton and Tyler had already arrived; we remained there for the Sunday, and embarked on Monday in a vessel which had been hired for the General and suite. On the same day we arrived at Ostend, and put up at an hotel in the square; where I was surprised to hear the General, in excellent French, get up a flirtation with our very pretty waiting-maid.

Sir Thomas Picton was a stern-looking, strong-built man, about the middle height, and considered very like the Hetman Platoff. He generally wore a blue frock-coat, very tightly buttoned up to the throat; a very large black silk neckcloth, showing little or no shirt-collar; dark trousers, boots, and a round hat: it was in this very dress that he was attired at Quatre Bras, as he had hurried off to the scene of action before his uniform arrived. After sleeping at Ostend, the General and Tyler went the next morning to Ghent, and on Thursday to Brussels. I proceeded by boat to Ghent, and, without stopping, hired a carriage, and arrived in time to order rooms for Sir Thomas at the Hotel d'Angleterre, Rue de la Madeleine, at Brussels: our horses followed us.

While we were at breakfast, Colonel Canning came to inform the General that the Duke of Wellington wished to see him immediately. Sir Thomas lost not a moment in obeying the order of his chief, leaving the breakfast-table and proceeding to the park, where Wellington was walking with Fitzroy Somerset and the Duke of Richmond. Picton's manner was always more familiar than the Duke liked in his lieutenants, and on this occasion he approached him in a careless sort of way, just as he might have met an equal. The Duke bowed coldly to him, and said, "I am glad you are come, Sir Thomas; the sooner you get on horseback the better; no time is to be lost. You will take the command of the troops in advance. The Prince of Orange knows by this time that you will go to his assistance." Picton appeared not to like the Duke's manner; for, when he bowed and left, he muttered a few words which convinced those who were with him that he was not much pleased with his interview.

QUATRE BRAS

I got upon the best of my two horses, and followed Sir Thomas Picton and his staff to Quatre Bras at full speed. His division was already engaged in supporting the Prince of Orange, and had deployed itself in two lines in front of the road to Sombref when he arrived. Sir Thomas immediately took the command. Shortly afterwards, Kempt's and Pack's brigades arrived by the Brussels road, and part of Alten's division by the Nivelles road.

Ney was very strong in cavalry, and our men were constantly formed into squares to receive them. The famous Kellerman, the hero of Marengo, tried a last charge, and was very nearly being taken or killed, as his horse was shot under him when very near us. Wellington at last took the offensive;--a charge was made against the French, which succeeded, and we remained masters of the field. I acted as a mere spectator, and got, on one occasion, just within twenty or thirty yards of some of the cuirassiers; but my horse was too quick for them.

On the 17th, Wellington retreated upon Waterloo, about eleven o'clock. The infantry were masked by the cavalry in two lines, parallel to the Namur road. Our cavalry retired on the approach of the French cavalry, in three columns, on the Brussels road. A torrent of rain fell, upon the Emperor's ordering the heavy cavalry to charge us; while the fire of sixty or eighty pieces of cannon showed that we had chosen our position at Waterloo. Chambers said to me, "Now, Gronow, the loss has been very severe in the Guards, and I think you ought to go and see whether you are wanted; for, as you have really nothing to do with Picton, you had better join your regiment, or you may get into a scrape." Taking his advice, I rode off to where the Guards were stationed; the officers--amongst whom I remember Colonel Thomas and Brigade-Major Miller--expressed their astonishment and amazement on seeing me, and exclaimed, "What the deuce brought you here? Why are you not with your battalion in London? Get off your horse, and explain how you came here!"

Things were beginning to look a little awkward, when Gunthorpe, the adjutant, a great friend of mine, took my part and said, "As he is here, let us make the most of him; there's plenty of work for everyone. Come, Gronow, you shall go with the Hon. Captain Clements and a detachment to the village of Waterloo, to take charge of the French prisoners." I said, "What the deuce shall I do with my horse?" Upon which the Hon. Captain Stopford, aide-de-camp to Sir John Byng, volunteered to buy him. Having thus once more become a foot soldier, I started according to orders, and arrived at Waterloo.

GENERAL APPEARANCE OF THE FIELD OF WATERLOO

The day on which the battle of Waterloo was fought seemed to have been chosen by some providential accident for which human wisdom is unable to account. On the morning of the 18th the sun shone most gloriously, and so clear was the atmosphere that we could see the long, imposing lines of the enemy most distinctly. Immediately in front of the division to which I belonged, and, I should imagine, about half a mile from us, were posted cavalry and artillery; and to the right and left the French had already engaged us, attacking Huguemont and La Haye Sainte. We heard incessantly the measured boom of artillery, accompanied by the incessant rattling echoes of musketry.

The whole of the British infantry not actually engaged were at that time formed into squares; and as you looked along our lines, it seemed as if we formed a continuous wall of human beings. I recollect distinctly being able to see Bonaparte and his staff; and some of my brother officers using the glass, exclaimed, "There he is on his white horse." I should not forget to state that when the enemy's artillery began to play on us, we had orders to lie down, when we could hear the shot and shell whistling around us, killing and wounding great numbers; then again we were ordered on our knees to receive cavalry. The French artillery--which consisted of three hundred guns, though we did not muster more than half that number--committed terrible havoc during the early part of the battle, whilst we were acting on the defensive.

THE DUKE OF WELLINGTON IN OUR SQUARE

About four P.M. the enemy's artillery in front of us ceased firing all of a sudden, and we saw large masses of cavalry advance: not a man present who survived could have forgotten in after life the awful grandeur of that charge. You discovered at a distance what appeared to be an overwhelming, long moving line, which, ever advancing, glittered like a stormy wave of the sea when it catches the sunlight. On they came until they got near enough, whilst the very earth seemed to vibrate beneath the thundering tramp of the mounted host. One might suppose that nothing could have resisted the shock of this terrible moving mass. They were the famous cuirassiers, almost all old soldiers, who had distinguished themselves on most of the battlefields of Europe. In an almost incredibly short period they were within twenty yards of us, shouting "Vive l'Empereur!" The word of command, "Prepare to receive cavalry," had been given, every man in the front ranks knelt, and a wall bristling with steel, held together by steady hands, presented itself to the infuriated cuirassiers.

I should observe that just before this charge the duke entered by one of the angles of the square, accompanied only by one aide-de-camp; all the rest of his staff being either killed or wounded. Our commander-in-chief, as far as I could judge, appeared perfectly composed; but looked very thoughtful and pale. He was dressed in a grey great-coat with a cape, white cravat, leather pantaloons, Hessian boots, and a large cocked hat a la Russe.

The charge of the French cavalry was gallantly executed; but our well-directed fire brought men and horses down, and ere long the utmost confusion arose in their ranks. The officers were exceedingly brave, and by their gestures and fearless bearing did all in their power to encourage their men to form again and renew the attack. The duke sat unmoved, mounted on his favourite charger. I recollect his asking the Hon. Lieut.-Colonel Stanhope what o'clock it was, upon which Stanhope took out his watch, and said it was twenty minutes past four. The Duke replied, "The battle is mine; and if the Prussians arrive soon, there will be an end of the war."

THE FRENCH CAVALRY CHARGING THE BRUNSWICKERS

Soon after the cuirassiers had retired, we observed to our right the red hussars of the Garde Imperiale charging a square of Brunswick riflemen, who were about fifty yards from us. This charge was brilliantly executed, but the well-sustained fire from the square baffled the enemy, who were obliged to retire after suffering a severe loss in killed and wounded. The ground was completely covered with those brave men, who lay in various positions, mutilated in every conceivable way. Among the fallen we perceived the gallant colonel of the hussars lying under his horse, which had been killed, All of a sudden two riflemen of the Brunswickers left their battalion, and after taking from their helpless victim his purse, watch, and other articles of value, they deliberately put the colonel's pistols to the poor fellow's head and blew out his brains. "Shame! shame!" was heard from our ranks, and a feeling of indignation ran through the whole line; but the deed was done: this brave soldier lay a lifeless corpse in sight of his cruel foes, whose only excuse perhaps was that their sovereign, the Duke of Brunswick, had been killed two days before by the French.

Again and again various cavalry regiments, heavy dragoons, lancers, hussars, carabineers of the Guard, endeavoured to break our walls of steel. The enemy's cavalry had to advance over ground which was so heavy that they could not reach us except at a trot; they therefore came upon us in a much more compact mass than they probably would have done if the ground had been more favourable. When they got within ten or fifteen yards they discharged their carbines, to the cry of "Vive l' Empereur!" their fire produced little effect, as that of cavalry generally does. Our men had orders not to fire unless they could do so on a near mass; the object being to economize our ammunition, and not to waste it on scattered soldiers. The result was, that when the cavalry had discharged their carbines, and were still far off, we occasionally stood face to face, looking at each other inactively, not knowing what the next move might be. The lancers were particularly troublesome, and approached us with the utmost daring. On one occasion I remember, the enemy's artillery having made a gap in the square, the lancers were evidently waiting to avail themselves of it, to rush among us, when Colonel Staples at once observing their intention, with the utmost promptness filled up the gap, and thus again completed our impregnable steel wall; but in this act he fell mortally wounded. The cavalry seeing this, made no attempt to carry out their original intentions, and observing that we had entirely regained our square, confined themselves to hovering round us. I must not forget to mention that the lancers in particular never failed to despatch our wounded whenever they had an opportunity of doing so.

When we received cavalry, the order was to fire low; so that on the first discharge of musketry the ground was strewed with the fallen horses and their riders, which impeded the advance of those behind them and broke the shock of the charge. It was pitiable to witness the agony of the poor horses, who really seemed conscious of the dangers that surrounded them: we often saw a poor wounded animal raise its head, as if looking for its rider to afford him aid. There is nothing perhaps amongst the episodes of a great battle more striking than the debris of a cavalry charge, where men and horses are seen scattered and wounded on the ground in every variety of painful attitude. Many a time the heart sickened at the moaning tones of agony which came from man and scarcely less intelligent horse, as they lay in fearful agony upon the field of battle.

THE LAST CHARGE AT WATERLOO

It was about five o'clock on that memorable day, that we suddenly received orders to retire behind an elevation in our rear. The enemy's artillery had come up en masse within a hundred yards of us. By the time they began to discharge their guns, however, we were lying down behind the rising ground, and protected by the ridge before referred to. The enemy's cavalry was in the rear of their artillery, in order to be ready to protect it if attacked; but no attempt was made on our part to do so. After they had pounded away at us for about half an hour, they deployed, and up came the whole mass of the Imperial infantry of the Guard, led on by the Emperor in person. We had now before us probably about 20,000 of the best soldiers in France, the heroes of many memorable victories; we saw the bearskin caps rising higher and higher as they ascended the ridge of ground which separated us, and advanced nearer and nearer to our lines. It was at this moment the Duke of Wellington gave his famous order for our bayonet charge, as he rode along the line: these are the precise words he made use of--"Guards, get up and charge!" We were instantly on our legs, and after so many hours of inaction and irritation at maintaining a purely defensive attitude--all the time suffering the loss of comrades and friends--the spirit which animated officers and men may easily be imagined. After firing a volley as soon as the enemy were within shot, we rushed on with fixed bayonets, and that hearty hurrah peculiar to British soldiers.

It appeared that our men, deliberately and with calculation, singled out their victims; for as they came upon the Imperial Guard our line broke, and the fighting became irregular. The impetuosity of our men seemed almost to paralyze their enemies: I witnessed several of the Imperial Guard who were run through the body apparently without any resistance on their parts. I observed a big Welshman of the name of Hughes, who was six feet seven inches in height, run through with his bayonet, and knock down with the butt end of his firelock, I should think a dozen at least of his opponents. This terrible contest did not last more than ten minutes, for the Imperial Guard was soon in full retreat, leaving all their guns and many prisoners in our hands. The famous General Cambronne was taken prisoner fighting hand to hand with the gallant Sir Colin Halkett, who was shortly after shot through the cheeks by a grape-shot. Cambronne's supposed answer of "La Garde ne se rend pas" was an invention of after-times, and he himself always denied having used such an expression.

HUGUEMONT

Early on the morning after the battle of Waterloo, I visited Huguemont, in order to witness with my own eyes the traces of one of the most hotly-contested spots of the field of battle. I came first upon the orchard, and there discovered heaps of dead men, in various uniforms: those of the Guards in their usual red jackets, the German Legion in green, and the French dressed in blue, mingled together. The dead and the wounded positively covered the whole area of the orchard; not less than two thousand men had there fallen. The apple-trees presented a singular appearance; shattered branches were seen hanging about their mother-trunks in such profusion that one might almost suppose the stiff-growing and stunted tree had been converted into the willow: every tree was riddled and smashed in a manner which told that the showers of shot had been incessant. On this spot I lost some of my dearest and bravest friends, and the country had to mourn many of its most heroic sons slain here.

I must observe that, according to the custom of commanding officers, whose business it is after a great battle to report to the Commander-in-Chief, the muster-roll of fame always closes before the rank of captain. It has always appeared to me a great injustice that there should ever be any limit to the roll of gallantry of either officers or men. If a captain, lieutenant, an ensign, a sergeant, or a private, has distinguished himself for his bravery, his intelligence, or both, their deeds ought to be reported, in order that the sovereign and nation should know who really fight the great battles of England. Of the class of officers and men to which I have referred, there were many of even superior rank who were omitted to be mentioned in the public despatches.

Thus, for example, to the individual courage of Lord Saltoun and Charley Ellis, who commanded the light companies, was mainly owing our success at Huguemont. The same may be said of Needham, Percival, Erskine, Grant, Vyner, Buckley, Master, and young Algernon Greville, who at that time could not have been more than seventeen years old. Excepting Percival, whose jaws were torn away by a grape-shot, everyone of these heroes miraculously escaped.

I do not wish, in making these observations, to detract from the bravery and skill of officers whose names have already been mentioned in official despatches, but I think it only just that the services of those I have particularized should not be forgotten by one of their companions in arms.

BYNG WITH HIS BRIGADE AT WATERLOO

No individual officer more distinguished himself than did General Byng at the battle of Waterloo. In the early part of the day he was seen at Huguemont, leading his men in the thick of the fight; later he was with the battalion in square, where his presence animated to the utmost enthusiasm both officers and men. It is difficult to imagine how this courageous man passed through such innumerable dangers from shot and shell without receiving a single wound. I must also mention some other instances of courage and devotion in officers belonging to this brigade; for instance, it was Colonel MacDonell, a man of colossal stature, with Hesketh, Bowes, Tom Sowerby, and Hugh Seymour, who commanded from the inside the Chateau of Huguemont. When the French had taken possession of the orchard, they made a rush at the principal door of the chateau, which had been turned into a fortress. MacDonell and the above officers placed themselves, accompanied by some of their men, behind the portal and prevented the French from entering. Amongst other officers of that brigade who were most conspicuous for bravery, I would record the names of Montague, the "vigorous Gooch," as he was called, and the well-known Jack Standen.

THE LATE DUKE OF RICHMOND

One of the most intimate friends of the Duke of Wellington was the Earl of March, afterwards Duke of Richmond. He was a genuine hard-working soldier, a man of extraordinary courage, and one who was ever found ready to gain laurels amidst the greatest dangers. When the 7th Fusiliers crossed the Bidassoa, the late duke left the staff and joined the regiment in which he had a company. At Orthes, in the thick of the fight, he received a shot which passed through his lungs; from this severe wound he recovered sufficiently to be able to join the Duke of Wellington, to whom he was exceedingly useful at the battle of Waterloo. On his return to England, he united himself to the most remarkably beautiful girl of the day, the eldest daughter of Lord Anglesea, and whose mother was the lovely Duchess of Argyle.

THE UNFORTUNATE CHARGE OF THE HOUSEHOLD BRIGADE

When Lord Uxbridge gave orders to Sir W. Ponsonby and Lord Edward Somerset to charge the enemy, our cavalry advanced with the greatest bravery, cut through everything in their way, and gallantly attacked whole regiments of infantry; but eventually they came upon a masked battery of twenty guns, which carried death and destruction through our ranks, and our poor fellows were obliged to give way. The French cavalry followed on their retreat, when, perhaps, the severest hand-to-hand cavalry fighting took place within the memory of man. The Duke of Wellington was perfectly furious that this arm had been engaged without his orders, and lost not a moment in sending them to the rear, where they remained during the rest of the day. This disaster gave the French cavalry an opportunity of annoying and insulting us, and compelled the artillerymen to seek shelter in our squares; and if the French had been provided with tackle, or harness of any description, our guns would have been taken. It is, therefore, not to be wondered at that the Duke should have expressed himself in no measured terms about the cavalry movements referred to. I recollect that, when his grace was in our square, our soldiers were so mortified at seeing the French deliberately walking their horses between our regiment and those regiments to our right and left, that they shouted, "Where are our cavalry? why don't they come and pitch into those French fellows?"

THE DUKE OF WELLINGTON'S OPINION OF THE FRENCH CAVALRY

A day or two after our arrival in Paris from Waterloo, Colonel Felton Hervey having entered the dining-room with the despatches which had come from London, the Duke asked, "What news have you, Hervey?" upon which, Colonel Felton Hervey answered, "I observe by the Gazette that the Prince Regent has made himself Captain-General of the Life Guards and Blues, for their brilliant conduct at Waterloo."

"Ah!" replied the Duke, "his Royal Highness is our Sovereign, and can do what he pleases; but this I will say, the cavalry of other European armies have won victories for their generals, but mine have invariably got me into scrapes. It is true that they have always fought gallantly and bravely, and have generally got themselves out of their difficulties by sheer pluck."

The justice of this observation has since been confirmed by the charge at Balaklava, where our cavalry undauntedly rushed into the face of death under the command of that intrepid officer Lord Cardigan.

MARSHAL EXCELMANN'S OPINION OF THE BRITISH CAVALRY

Experience has taught me that there is nothing more valuable than the opinions of intelligent foreigners on the military and naval excellences, and the failures, of our united service. Marshal Excelmann's opinion about the British cavalry struck me as remarkably instructive: he used to say, "Your horses are the finest in the world, and your men ride better than any Continental soldiers; with such materials, the English cavalry ought to have done more than has ever been accomplished by them on the field of battle. The great deficiency is in your officers, who have nothing to recommend them but their dash and sitting well in their saddles; indeed, as far as my experience goes, your English generals have never understood the use of cavalry: they have undoubtedly frequently misapplied that important arm of a grand army, and have never, up to the battle of Waterloo, employed the mounted soldier at the proper time and in the proper place. The British cavalry officer seems to be impressed with the conviction that he can dash and ride over everything; as if the art of war were precisely the same as that of fox-hunting. I need not remind you of the charge of your two heavy brigades at Waterloo: this charge was utterly useless, and all the world knows they came upon a masked battery, which obliged a retreat, and entirely disconcerted Wellington's plans during the rest of the day."

"Permit me," he added, "to point out a gross error as regards the dress of your cavalry. I have seen prisoners so tightly habited that it was impossible for them to use their sabres with facility." The French Marshal concluded by observing--"I should wish nothing better than such material as your men and horses are made of; since with generals who wield cavalry, and officers who are thoroughly acquainted with that duty in the field, I do not hesitate to say I might gain a battle."

Such was the opinion of a man of cool judgment, and one of the most experienced cavalry officers of the day.

APPEARANCE OF PARIS WHEN THE ALLIES ENTERED

I propose giving my own impression of the aspect of Paris and its vicinity when our regiment entered that city on the 25th of June, 1815. I recollect we marched from the plain of St. Denis, my battalion being about five hundred strong, the survivors of the heroic fight of the 18th of June. We approached near enough to be within fire of the batteries of Montmartre, and bivouacked for three weeks in the Bois de Boulogne. That now beautiful garden was at the period to which I refer a wild pathless wood, swampy, and entirely neglected. The Prussians, who were in bivouac near us, amused themselves by doing as much damage as they could, without any useful aim or object: they cut down the finest trees, and set the wood on fire at several points. There were about three thousand of the Guards then encamped in the wood, and I should think about ten thousand Prussians. Our camp was not remarkable for its courtesy towards them; in fact, our intercourse was confined to the most ordinary demands of duty, as allies in an enemy's country.

I believe I was one of the first of the British army who penetrated into the heart of Paris after Waterloo. I entered by the Porte Maillot, and passed the Arc de Triomphe, which was then building. In those days the Champs Elysees only contained a few scattered houses, and the roads and pathways were ancle deep in mud. The only attempt at lighting was the suspension of a few lamps on cords, which crossed the roads. Here I found the Scotch regiments bivouacking; their peculiar uniform created a considerable sensation amongst the Parisian women, who did not hesitate to declare that the want of culottes was most indecent. I passed through the camp, and proceeded on towards the gardens of the Tuilleries. This ancient palace of the Kings of France presented, so far as the old front is concerned, the same aspect that it does at the present day; but there were then no flower-gardens, although the same stately rows of trees which now ornament the grounds were then in their midsummer verdure.

Being in uniform, I created an immense amount of curiosity amongst the Parisians; who, by the way, I fancied regarded me with no loving looks. The first house

I entered was a cafe in the garden of the Tuilleries, called Legac's. I there met a man who told me he was by descent an Englishman; though he had been born in Paris, and had really never quitted France. He approached me, saying, "Sir, I am delighted to see an English officer in Paris, and you are the first I have yet met with." He talked about the battle of Waterloo, and gave me some useful directions concerning restaurants and cafes. Along the Boulevards were handsome houses, isolated, with gardens interspersed, and the roads were bordered on both sides with stately, spreading trees, some of them probably a hundred years old. There was but an imperfect pavement, the stepping-stones of which were adapted to display the Parisian female ankle and boot in all their calculated coquetry; and the road showed nothing but mother earth, in the middle of which a dirty gutter served to convey the impurities of the city to the river. The people in the streets appeared sulky and stupefied: here and there I noticed groups of the higher classes evidently discussing the events of the moment.

How strange humanity would look in our day in the costume of the first empire. The ladies wore very scanty and short skirts, which left little or no waist; their bonnets were of exaggerated proportions, and protruded at least a foot from their faces, and they generally carried a fan. The men wore blue or black coats, which were baggily made, and reached down to their ankles; their hats were enormously large, and spread out at the top.

I dined the first day of my entrance into Paris at the Cafe Anglais, on the Boulevard des Italiens, where I found to my surprise several of my brother officers. I recollect the charge for the dinner was about one-third what it would be at the present day. I had a potage, fish--anything but fresh, and, according to English predilections and taste, of course I ordered a beef-steak and pommes de terre. The wine, I thought, was sour. The dinner cost about two francs. The theatres at this time, as may easily be imagined, were not very well attended. I recollect going to the Francais, where I saw for the first time the famous Talma. There was but a scanty audience; in fact all the best places in the house were empty.

It may easily be imagined that, at a moment like this, most of those who had a stake in the country were pondering over the great and real drama that was then taking place. Napoleon had fled to Rochfort; the wreck of his army had retreated beyond the Loire; no list of killed and wounded had appeared; and, strange to say, the official journal of Paris had made out that the great Imperial army at Waterloo had gained a victory. There were, nevertheless, hundreds of people in Paris who knew to the contrary, and many were already aware that they had lost relations and friends in the great battle.

Louis XVIII. arrived, as well as I can remember, at the Tuileries on the 26th of July, 1815, and his reception by the Parisians was a singular illustration of the versatile character of the French nation, and the sudden and often inexplicable changes which take place in the feeling of the populace. When the Bourbon, in his old lumbering state carriage, drove down the Boulevards, accompanied by the Garde du Corps, the people in the streets and at the windows displayed the wildest joy, enthusiastically shouting "Vive le Roi!" amidst the waving of hats and handkerchiefs, while white sheets or white rags were made to do the duty of a Bourbon banner. The king was dressed in a blue coat with a red collar, and wore also a white waistcoat and a cocked hat with a white cockade in it. His portly and good-natured appearance seemed to be appreciated by the crowd, whom he saluted with a benevolent smile. I should here mention that two great devotees of the Church sat opposite to the King on this memorable occasion. The cortege proceeded slowly down the Rue de la Paix until the Tuileries was reached, where a company of the Guards, together with a certain number of the Garde Nationale of Paris, were stationed.

It fell to my lot to be on duty the day after, when the Duke of Wellington and Lord Castlereagh arrived to pay their respects to the restored monarch. I happened to be in the Salle des Marechaux when these illustrious personages passed through that magnificent apartment. The respect paid to the Duke of Wellington on this occasion may be easily imagined, from the fact that a number of ladies of the highest rank, and of course partisans of the legitimate dynasty, formed an avenue through which the hero of Waterloo passed, exchanging with them courteous recognitions. The King was waiting in the grand reception apartment to receive the great British captain. The interview, I have every reason to believe, was not confined to the courtesies of the palace.

The position of the Duke was a difficult one. In the first place, he had to curb the vindictive vandalism of Blucher and his army, who would have levelled the city of Paris to the ground, if they could have done so; on the other hand, he had to practise a considerable amount of diplomacy towards the newly-restored King. At the same time the Duke's powers from his own Government were necessarily limited. A spirit of vindictiveness pervaded the restored Court against Napoleon and his adherents, which the Duke constantly endeavoured to modify. I must not forget to give an illustration of this state of feeling. It was actually proposed by Talleyrand, Fouche, and some important ecclesiastics of the ultra-royalist party, to arrest and shoot the Emperor Napoleon, who was then at Rochfort: so anxious were they to commit this criminal, inhuman, and cowardly act, on an illustrious fallen enemy, who had made the arms of France glorious throughout Europe, that they suggested to the Duke, who had the command of the old wooden-armed semaphores, to employ the telegraph to order what I should have designated by no other name than the assassination of the Caesar of modern history.

MARSHAL NEY AND WELLINGTON

As an illustration of the false impressions which are always disseminated concerning public men, I must record the following fact:--The Duke of Wellington was accused of being implicated in the military murder of Ney. Now, so far from this being the truth, I know positively that the Duke of Wellington used every endeavour to prevent this national disgrace; but the Church party, ever crafty and ever ready to profit by the weakness and passions of humanity, supported the King in his moments of excited revenge. It is a lamentable fact, but no less historical truth, that the Roman Catholic Church has ever sought to make the graves of its enemies the foundations of its power. The Duke of Wellington was never able to approach the King or use his influence to save Marshal Ney's life; but everything he could do was done, in order to accomplish his benevolent views. I repeat, the influence of the ultra-montane party triumphed over the Christian humanity of the illustrious Duke.

THE PALAIS ROYAL AFTER THE RESTORATION

France has often been called the centre of European fashion and gaiety; and the Palais Royal, at the period to which I refer, might be called the very heart of French dissipation. It was a theatre in which all the great actors of fashion of all nations met to play their parts: on this spot were congregated daily an immense multitude, for no other purpose than to watch the busy comedy of real life that animated the corridors, gardens, and saloons of that vast building, which was founded by Richelieu and Mazarin, and modified by Philippe Egalite. Mingled together, and moving about the area of this oblong-square block of buildings, might be seen, about seven o'clock P.M., a crowd of English, Russian, Prussian, Austrian, and other officers of the Allied armies, together with countless foreigners from all parts of the world. Here, too, might have been seen the present King of Prussia, with his father and brother, the late king, the Dukes of Nassau, Baden, and a host of continental princes, who entered familiarly into the amusements of ordinary mortals, dining incog. at the most renowned restaurants, and flirting with painted female frailty.

A description of one of the houses of the Palais Royal, will serve to portray the whole of this French pandemonium. On the ground floor is a jeweller's shop, where may be purchased diamonds, pearls, emeralds, and every description of female ornament, such as only can be possessed by those who have very large sums of money at their command. It was here that the successful gambler often deposited a portion of his winnings, and took away some costly article of jewellery, which he presented to some female friend who had never appeared with him at the altar of marriage. Beside this shop was a staircase, generally very dirty, which communicated with the floors above. Immediately over the shop was a cafe, at the counter of which presided a lady, generally of more than ordinary female attractions, who was very much decolletee, and wore an amount of jewellery which would have made the eye of an Israelite twinkle with delight. And there la creme de la creme of male society used to meet, sip their ice and drink their cup of mocha, whilst holding long conversations, almost exclusively about gambling and women.

Men's thoughts, in this region, seemed to centre night and day upon the tapis vert, and at the entrance of this salon was that fatal chamber, over which might have been written the famous line of Dante, "Voi che entrate lasciate ogni speranza." The reader will at once understand that I am referring to the gambling-house, the so-called "hell" of modern society. In one room was the rouge et noir table, which, from the hour of twelve in the morning, was surrounded by men in every stage of the gambling malady. There was the young pigeon, who, on losing his first feather, had experienced an exciting sensation which, if followed by a bit of good luck, gave him a confidence that the parasites around him, in order to flatter his vanity, would call pluck. There were others in a more advanced stage of the fever, who had long since lost the greater part of their incomes, having mortgaged their property, and been in too frequent correspondence with the Jews. These men had not got to the last stage of gambling despair, but they were so far advanced on the road to perdition that their days were clouded by perpetual anxiety, which reproduced itself in their very dreams. The gambler who has thus far advanced in his career, lives in an inferno of his own creation: the charms of society, the beauty of woman, the attractions of the fine arts, and even the enjoyment of a good dinner, are to him rather a source of irritation than delight. The confirmed gamester is doing nothing less than perpetually digging a grave for his own happiness.

The third and most numerous group of men round the tapis vert consisted of a class most of whom had already spent their fortunes, exhausted their health, and lost their position in society, by the fatal and demoralizing thirst for gold, which still fascinated them. These became the hawks of the gambling table; their quick and wild-glancing eyes were constantly looking out for suitable game during the day, and leaving it where it might be bagged at night. Both at the rouge et noir table and roulette the same sort of company might be met with. These gambling-houses were the very fountains of immorality: they gathered together, under the most seductive circumstances, the swindler and the swindled. There were tables for all classes--the workman might play with 20 sous, or the gentleman with 10,000 francs. The law did not prevent any class from indulging in a vice that assisted to fill the coffers of the municipality of Paris.

The floor over the gambling-house was occupied by unmarried women. I will not attempt to picture some of the saddest evils of the society of large cities; but I may add that these Phrynes lived in a style of splendour which can only be accounted for by the fact of their participating in the easily-earned gains of the gambling-house regime. Such was the state of the Palais Royal under Louis XVIII. and Charles X.: the Palais Royal of the present day is simply a tame and legitimately-commercial mart, compared with that of olden times. Society has changed; Government no longer patronizes such nests of immorality; and though vice may exist to the same extent, it assumes another garb, and does not appear in the open streets, as at the period to which I have referred.

At that time, the Palais Royal was externally the only well-lighted place in Paris. It was the rendezvous of all idlers, and especially of that particular class of ladies who lay out their attractions for the public at large. These were to be seen at all hours in full dress, their bare necks ornamented with mock diamonds and pearls; and thus decked out in all their finery, they paraded up and down, casting their eyes significantly on every side. Some strange stories are told in connection with the gambling houses of the Palais Royal. An officer of the Grenadier Guards came to Paris on leave of absence, took apartments here, and never left it until his time of absence had expired. On his arrival in London one of his friends inquired whether this was true, to which he replied, "Of course it is; for I found everything I wanted there, both for body and mind."

THE ENGLISH IN PARIS AFTER THE RESTORATION OF THE BOURBONS

There is no more ordinary illusion belonging to humanity than that which enables us to discover, in the fashions of the day, an elegance and comeliness of dress which a few years after we ourselves regard as odious caricatures of costume. Thousands of oddly-dressed English flocked to Paris immediately after the war: I remember that the burden of one of the popular songs of the day was, "All the world's in Paris;" and our countrymen and women having so long been excluded from French modes, had adopted fashions of their own quite as remarkable and eccentric as those of the Parisians, and much less graceful. British beauties were dressed in long, strait pelisses of various colours; the body of the dress was never of the same colour as the skirt; and the bonnet was of the bee-hive shape, and very small. The characteristic of the dress of the gentleman was a coat of light blue, or snuff-colour, With brass buttons, the tail reaching nearly to the heels; a gigantic bunch of seals dangled from his fob, whilst his pantaloons were short and tight at the knees; and a spacious waistcoat, with a voluminous muslin cravat and a frilled shirt, completed the toilette. The dress of the British military, in its stiff and formal ugliness, was equally cumbrous and ludicrous.

Lady Oxford--that beautiful and accomplished woman, who lived in her hotel in the Rue de Clichy--gave charming soirees, at which were gathered the elite of Paris society. Among these were Edward Montague, Charles Standish, Hervey Aston, Arthur Upton, "Kangaroo" Cook, Benjamin Constant, Dupin, Casimir Perier, as well as the chief Orleanists. On one occasion, I recollect seeing there George Canning and the celebrated Madame de Stael. Cornwall, the eldest son of the Bishop of Worcester, had, from some unaccountable cause, a misunderstanding with Madame de Stael, who appeared very excited, and said to Lady Oxford, in a loud voice, "Notre ami, M. Cornewal, est grosso, rosso, e furioso." It should be observed that the gentleman thus characterized was red-haired, and hasty in temper. All who heard this denunciation were astounded at the lady's manner, for she looked daggers at the object of her sarcasm.

Fox, the secretary of the embassy, was an excellent man, but odd, indolent, and careless in the extreme; he was seldom seen in the daytime, unless it was either at the embassy in a state of negligee, or in bed. At night he used to go to the Salon des Etrangers; and, if he possessed a Napoleon, it was sure to be thrown away at hazard, or rouge et noir. On one occasion, however, fortune favoured him in a most extraordinary manner. The late Henry Baring having recommended him to take the dice-box, Fox replied, "I will do so for the last time, for all my money is thrown away upon this infernal table." Fox staked all he had in his pockets; he threw in eleven times, breaking the bank, and taking home for his share 60,000 francs. After this, several days passed without any tidings being heard of him; but upon my calling at the embassy to get my passport vised, I went into his room, and saw it filled with Cashmere shawls, silk, Chantilly veils, bonnets, gloves, shoes, and other articles of ladies' dress. On my asking the purpose of all this millinery, Fox replied, in a good-natured way, "Why, my dear Gronow, it was the only means to prevent those rascals at the salon winning back my money."

LES ANGLAISES POUR RIRE

An order had been given to the managers of all the theatres in Paris to admit a certain number of soldiers of the army of occupation, free of expense. It happened that a party of the Guards, composed of a sergeant and a few men, went to the Theatre des Varietes on the Boulevards, where one of the pieces, entitled Les Anglaises pour Rire, was admirably acted by Potier and Brunet. In this piece Englishwomen were represented in a very ridiculous light by those accomplished performers. This gave great offence to our soldiers, and the sergeant and his men determined to put a stop to the acting; accordingly they stormed the stage, and laid violent hands upon the actors, eventually driving them off. The police were called in, and foolishly wanted to take our men to prison; but they soon found to their cost that they had to deal with unmanageable opponents, for the whole posse of gendarmes were charged and driven out of the theatre. A crowd assembled on the Boulevards; which, however, soon dispersed when it became known that English soldiers were determined, coute qu'il coute, to prevent their countrywomen from being ridiculed. It must be remembered that the only revenge which the Parisians were able to take upon the conquerors was to ridicule them; and the English generally took it in good humour, and laughed at the extravagant drollery of the burlesque.

The English soldiers generally walked about Paris in parties of a dozen, and were quiet and well-behaved. They usually gathered every day on the Boulevard du Temple, where they were amused with the mountebanks and jugglers there assembled.

This part of Paris is now completely changed: but at the time I speak of, it was an extensive open place, where every species of fun was carried on, as at fairs: there were gambling, rope-dancing, wild beasts, and shows; booths for the sale of cakes, gingerbread, fruit, and lemonade; and every species of attraction that pleases the multitude; but that space has now been built upon, and these sports have all migrated to the barriers.

During the time our troops remained, we had only one man found dead in the streets: it was said that he had been murdered; but of that there was considerable doubt, for no signs of violence were found. This was strongly in contrast to what occurred to the Prussian soldiers. It was asserted, and, indeed, proved beyond a doubt, that numbers of them were assassinated; and in some parts of France it was not unusual to find in the morning, in deep wells or cellars, several bodies of soldiers of that nation who had been killed during the night; so strong was the hatred borne against them by the French.

COACHING AND RACING IN 1815

Stage-coaches, or four-in-hand teams, were introduced in Paris in 1815 by Captain Bacon, of the 10th Hussars (afterwards a general in the Portuguese service), Sir Charles Smith, Mr. Roles, the brewer, and Arnold, of the 10th. They used to meet opposite Demidoff's house, afterwards the Cafe de Paris, and drive to the Boulevard Beaumarchais, and then back again, proceeding to the then unfinished Arc du Triomphe. Crowds assembled to witness the departure of the teams; and it created no little amusement to the Parisian to see perched upon Sir C. Smith's coach one or two smartly-dressed ladies, who appeared quite at home. Sir Charles was likewise a great supporter of the turf, and was the first man who brought over from England thorough-bred horses. By his indefatigable energy he contrived to get up very fair racing in the neighbourhood of Valenciennes; his trainer at this time being Tom Hurst, who is now, I believe, at Chantilly; and all the officers of our several cavalry and infantry regiments contributed their efforts to make these races respectable in the eyes of foreigners. Be this as it may, they were superior to those in the Champs de Mars, though under the patronage of the King.

I shall not forget the first time I witnessed racing in Paris, for it was more like a review of Gensdarmes and National Guards; the course was kept by a forest of bayonets, while mounted police galloped after the running horses, and, in some instances, reached the goal before them. The Duc d' Angouleme, with the Duc de Guiche and the Prefet, were present; but there was only one small stand, opposite to a sentry-box where the judge was placed. The running, to say the least of it, was ridiculous: horses and riders fell; and the fete, as it was called, ended with a flourish of trumpets. Wonderful changes have taken place since that time, and at the Bois de Boulogne and at Chantilly may be seen running equal to that of our best races in England; and our neighbours produce horses, bred in France, that can carry off some of the great prizes in our own "Isthmian games."

PARISIAN CAFES IN 1815

At the present day, Paris may be said to be a city of cafes and restaurants. The railroads and steamboats enable the rich of every quarter of the globe to reach the most attractive of all European cities with comparative economy and facility. All foreigners arriving in Paris seem by instinct to rush to the restaurateurs', where strangers may be counted by tens of thousands. It is not surprising that we find in every important street these gaudy modern triclinia, which, I should observe, are as much frequented by a certain class of French people as by foreigners, for Paris is proverbially fond of dining out; in fact, the social intercourse may be said to take place more frequently in the public cafe than under the domestic roof.

In 1815, I need scarcely remark that the condition of the roads in Europe, and the enormous expense of travelling, made a visit to Paris a journey which could only be indulged in by a very limited and wealthy class of strangers. Hotels and cafes were then neither so numerous nor so splendid as at the present day: Meurice's Hotel was a very insignificant establishment in the Rue de l'Echiquier; and in the Rue de la Paix, at that time unfinished, there were but two or three hotels, which would not be considered even second-rate at the present time. The site of the Maison Dore, at the corner of the Rue Lafitte, was then occupied by a shabby building which went by the name of the Hotel d'Angleterre, and was kept by the popular and once beautiful Madame Dunan. The most celebrated restaurant was that of Beauvilliers, in the Rue de Richelieu; mirrors and a little gilding were the decorative characteristics of this house; the cuisine was far superior to that of any restaurateur of our day, and the wines were first-rate. Beauvilliers was also celebrated for his supreme de volaille, and for his cotelette a la Soubise. The company consisted of the most distinguished men of Paris; here were to be seen Chateaubriand, Bailly de Ferrette, the Dukes of Fitzjames, Rochefoucauld, and Grammont, and many other remarkable personages. It was the custom to go to the theatres after dinner, and then to the Salon des Etrangers, which was the Parisian Crockford's.

Another famous dining-house was the Rocher de Cancaille, in the Rue Mandar, kept by Borel, formerly one of the cooks of Napoleon. Here the cuisine was so refined that people were reported to have come over from England expressly for the purpose of enjoying it: indeed, Borel once showed me a list of his customers, amongst whom I found the names of Robespierre, Charles James Fox, and the Duke of Bedford. In the Palais Royal the still well-known Trois Freres Provenceaux was in vogue, and frequented much by the French officers; being celebrated chiefly for its wines and its Provence dishes: it was in the Palais Royal that General Lannes, Junot, Murat, and other distinguished officers, used to meet Bonaparte just before and during the Consulate; but the cafes, with the exception of the Mille Colonnes, were not nearly so smartly fitted-up as they now are. The Cafe Turc, on the Boulevard du Temple, latterly visited chiefly by shopkeepers, was much frequented: smoking was not allowed, and then, as now, ladies were seen here; more especially when the theatres had closed.

REVIEW OF THE ALLIED ARMIES BY THE ALLIED SOVEREIGNS IN PARIS

In July, 1815, it was agreed by the Sovereigns of Russia, Austria, Prussia, Bavaria, Wurtemberg, and a host of petty German Powers--who had become wonderfully courageous and enthusiastically devoted to England, a few hours after the Battle of Waterloo--that a grand review should be held on the plains of St. Denis, where the whole of the allied forces were to meet. Accordingly, at an early hour on a fine summer morning, there were seen issuing from the various roads which centre on the plains of St. Denis, numerous English, Russian, Prussian, and Austrian regiments of horse and foot, in heavy marching order, with their bands playing; and finally a mass of men, numbering not less than 200,000, took up their positions on the wide-spreading field. About twelve o'clock, the Duke of Wellington, commander-in-chief of the allied army, approached, mounted on a favourite charger; and, strange as it may appear, on his right was observed a lady in a plain riding-habit, who was no other than Lady Shelley, the wife of the late Sir John Shelley.

Immediately behind the Duke followed the Emperors of Austria, and Russia; the Kings of Prussia, Holland, Bavaria, and Wurtemberg; several German princes, and general officers; the whole forming one of the most illustrious and numerous staffs ever brought together. The Duke of Wellington, thus accompanied, took up his position, and began manoeuvering, with a facility and confidence which elicited the admiration of all the experienced soldiers around him. Being on duty near his grace, I had an opportunity of hearing Prince Schwartzenberg say to the Duke, "You are the only man who can so well play at this game." The review lasted two hours; then the men marching home to their quarters, through a crowd of spectators which included the whole population of Paris. The most mournful silence was observed throughout on the part of the French.

CONDUCT OF THE RUSSIAN AND PRUSSIAN SOLDIERS DURING THE OCCUPATION OF PARIS BY THE ALLIES

It is only just to say that the moderation shown by the British army, from the Duke of Wellington down to the private soldier, during our occupation of Paris, contrasted most favourably with that of the Russian and Prussian military. Whilst we simply did our duty, and were civil to all those with whom we came in contact, the Russians and Prussians were frequently most insubordinate, and never lost an opportunity of insulting a people whose armies had almost always defeated them on the day of battle. I remember one particular occasion, when the Emperor of Russia reviewed his Garde Imperiale, that the Cossacks actually charged the crowd, and inflicted wounds on the unarmed and inoffensive spectators. I recollect, too, a Prussian regiment displaying its bravery in the Rue St. Honore on a number of hackney coachmen; indeed, scarcely a day passed without outrages being committed by the Russian and Prussian soldiers on the helpless population of the lower orders.

THE BRITISH EMBASSY IN PARIS

England was represented at this period by Sir Charles Stuart, who was one of the most popular ambassadors Great Britain ever sent to Paris. He made himself acceptable to his countrymen, and paid as much attention to individual interests as to the more weighty duties of State. His attaches, as is always the case, took their tone and manner from their chief, and were not only civil and agreeable to all those who went to the Embassy, but knew everything and everybody, and were of great use to the ambassador, keeping him well supplied with information on whatever event might be taking place. The British Embassy, in those days, was a centre where you were sure to find all the English gentlemen in Paris collected, from time to time. Dinners, balls, and receptions, were given with profusion throughout the season: in fact, Sir Charles spent the whole of his private income in these noble hospitalities. England was then represented, as it always should be in France, by an ambassador who worthily expressed the intelligence, the amiability, and the wealth, of the great country to which he belonged. At the present day, the British Embassy emulates the solitude of a monastic establishment; with the exception, however, of that hospitality and courtesy which the traveller and stranger were wont to experience, even in monasteries.

ESCAPE OF LAVALETTE FROM PRISON

Few circumstances created a greater sensation than the escape of Lavalette from the Conciergerie, after he had been destined by the French Government to give employment to the guillotine. The means by which the prisoner avoided his fate and disappointed his enemies, produced a deep respect for the English character, and led the French to believe that, however much the Governments of France and England might be disposed to foster feelings either of friendship or of enmity, individuals could entertain the deepest sense of regard for each other, and that a chivalrous feeling of honour would urge them on to the exercise of the noblest feelings of our nature. This incident likewise had a salutary influence in preventing acts of cruelty and of bloodshed, which were doubtless contemplated by those in power.

Lavalette had been, under the Imperial Government, head of the Post Office, which place he filled on the return of the Bourbons; and when the Emperor Napoleon arrived from Elba, he continued still to be thus employed. Doubtless, on all occasions when opportunity presented itself, he did all in his power to serve his great master; to whom, indeed, he was allied by domestic ties, having married into the Beauharnais family. When Louis the Eighteenth returned to Paris after the battle of Waterloo, Lavalette and the unfortunate Marshal Ney were singled out as traitors to the Bourbon cause, and tried, convicted, and sentenced to death. The 26th of December was the day fixed for the execution of Lavalette, a man of high respectability and of great connections, whose only fault was fidelity to his chief. On the evening of the 21st, Madame Lavalette, accompanied by her daughter and her governess, Madame Dutoit, a lady of seventy years of age, presented herself at the Conciergerie, to take a last farewell of her husband. She arrived at the prison in a sedan chair. On this very day the Procureur-general had given an order that no one should be admitted without an order signed by himself; the greffier having, however, on previous occasions been accustomed to receive Madame Lavalette with the two ladies who now sought also to enter the cell, did not object to it; so these three ladies proposed to take coffee with Lavalette. The under gaoler was sent to a neighbouring cafe to obtain it, and during his absence Lavalette exchanged dresses with his wife. He managed to pass undetected out of the prison, accompanied by his daughter, and entered the chair in which Madame Lavalette had arrived; which, owing to the management of a faithful valet, had been placed so that no observation could be made of the person entering it. The bearers found the chair somewhat heavier than usual, but were ignorant of the change that had taken place, and were glad to find, after proceeding a short distance, that the individual within preferred walking home, and giving up the sedan to the young lady. On the greffier entering the cell, he quickly discovered the ruse, and gave the alarm; the under gaoler was despatched to stop the chair, but he was too late.

Lavalette had formed a friendship with a young Englishman of the name of Bruce; to whom he immediately had recourse, throwing himself upon his generosity and kind feeling for protection, which was unhesitatingly afforded. But as

Bruce could do nothing alone, he consulted two English friends who had shown considerable sympathy for the fate of Marshal Ney--men of liberal principles and undoubted honour, and both of them officers in the British service: these were Captain Hutchinson and General Sir Robert Wilson. To the latter was committed the most difficult task, that of conveying out of France the condemned prisoner; but for this achievement few men were better fitted than Sir Robert Wilson, a man of fertile imagination, ready courage, great assurance, and singular power of command over others; who spoke French well, and was intimately acquainted with the military habits of different nations.

Sir Robert Wilson's career was a singular one: he had commenced life an ardent enemy of Bonaparte, and it was upon his evidence, collected in Egypt and published to the world, that the great general was for a long time believed to have poisoned his wounded soldiers at Jaffa. Afterwards he was attached to the Allied Sovereigns in their great campaign; but upon his arrival in Paris, his views of public affairs became suddenly changed; he threw off the yoke of preconceived opinions, became an ardent liberal, and so continued to the last hours of his life. The cause of this sudden change of opinion has never been thoroughly known, but certain it is that on every occasion he supported liberal opinions with a firmness and courage that astonished those who had known him in his earlier days.

Sir Robert undertook, in the midst of great dangers and difficulties, to convey Lavalette out of France; having dressed him in the uniform of an English officer, and obtained a passport under a feigned name, he took him in a cabriolet past the barriers as far as Compiegne, where a carriage was waiting for them. They passed through sundry examinations at the fortified towns, but fortunately escaped; the great difficulty being that, owing to Lavalette's having been the director of the posts, his countenance was familiar to almost all the postmasters who supplied relays of horses. At Cambray three hours were lost, from the gates being shut, and at Valenciennes they underwent three examinations; but eventually they got out of France. The police, however, became acquainted with the fact that Lavalette had been concealed in the Rue de Helder for three days, at the apartments of Mr. Bruce, and this enabled them to trace all the circumstances, showing that it was at the apartments of Hutchinson that Lavalette had changed his dress, and that he had remained there the night before he quitted Paris. The consequence was that Sir Robert Wilson,

Bruce, and Hutchinson, were tried for aiding the escape of a prisoner; and each of them was condemned to three months' imprisonment: the under-gaoler, who had evidently been well paid for services rendered, had two years' confinement allotted to him. I went to see Sir Robert Wilson during his stay in the Conciergerie--a punishment not very difficult to bear, but which marked him as a popular hero for his life. A circumstance I remember made a strong impression on me, proving that, however great may be the courage of a man in trying circumstances, a trifling incident might severely shake his nerves. I was accompanied by a favourite dog of the Countess of Oxford, who, not being aware of the high character of Sir Robert, or dissatisfied with his physiognomy, or for some good canine reason, took a sudden antipathy, and inserted his teeth into a somewhat fleshy part, but without doing much injury. The effect, however, on the General was extraordinary: he was most earnest to have the dog killed; but being certain that the animal was in no way diseased, I avoided obeying his wishes, and fear that I thus lost the good graces of the worthy man.

DUELLING IN FRANCE IN 1815

When the restoration of the Bourbons took place, a variety of circumstances combined to render duelling so common, that scarcely a day passed without one at least of these hostile meetings. Amongst the French themselves there were two parties always ready to distribute to each other "des coups d'epees"--the officers of Napoleon's army and the Bourbonist officers of the Garde du Corps. Then, again, there was the irritating presence of the English, Russian, Prussian, and Austrian officers in the French capital. In the duels between these soldiers and the French, the latter were always the aggressors. At Tortoni's, on the Boulevards, there was a room set apart for such quarrelsome gentlemen, where, after these meetings, they indulged in riotous champagne breakfasts. At this cafe might be seen all the most notorious duellists, amongst whom I can call to mind an Irishman in the Garde du Corps, W--, who was a most formidable fire-eater. The number of duels in which he had been engaged would seem incredible in the present day: he is said to have killed nine of his opponents in one year!

The Marquis de H--, descended of an ancient family in Brittany, also in the Garde du Corps, likewise fought innumerable duels, killing many of his antagonists. I have heard that on entering the army he was not of a quarrelsome disposition, but was laughed at, and bullied into fighting by his brother officers; and, like a wild beast that had once smelt blood, from the day of his first duel he took a delight in such fatal scenes--being ever ready to rush at and quarrel with any one. The marquis has now, I am glad to say, subsided into a very quiet, placable, and peacemaking old gentleman; but at the time I speak of he was much blamed for his duel with F--, a young man of nineteen. While dining at a cafe he exclaimed, "J'ai envie de tuer quelq'un," and rushed out into the street and to the theatres, trying to pick a quarrel; but he was so well known that no one was found willing to encounter him. At last, at the Theatre de la Porte St. Martin, he grossly insulted this young man, who was, I think, an eleve of the Ecole Polytechnique, and a duel took place, under the lamp-post near the theatre, with swords. He ran F-- through the body, and left him dead upon the ground.

The late Marshal St. A-- and General J-- were great duellists at this time, with a whole host of others whose names I forget. The meetings generally took place in the Bois de Boulogne, and the favourite weapon of the French was the small sword, or the sabre; but foreigners, in fighting with the French, who were generally capital swordsmen, availed themselves of the use of pistols. The ground for a duel with pistols was marked out by indicating two spots, which were twenty-five paces apart; the seconds then generally proceeded to toss up who should have the first shot; when the principals were placed, and the word was given to fire.

The Cafe Foy, in the Palais Royal, was the principal place of rendezvous for the Prussian officers, and to this cafe the French officers on half-pay frequently proceeded in order to pick quarrels with their foreign invaders; swords were quickly drawn, and frequently the most bloody frays took place: these originated not in any personal hatred, but from national jealousy on the part of the French, who could not bear the sight of foreign soldiers in their capital; which, ruled by the great captain of the age, had, like Rome, influenced the rest of the world. On one occasion our Guards, who were on duty at the Palais Royal, were called out to put an end to one of these encounters, in which fourteen Prussians and ten Frenchmen were either killed or wounded.

The French took every opportunity of insulting the English; and very frequently, I am sorry to say, those insults were not met in a manner to do honour to our character, Our countrymen in general were very pacific; but the most awkward customer the French ever came across was my fellow-countryman the late gallant Colonel Sir Charles S--, of the Engineers, who was ready for them with anything: sword, pistols, sabre, or fists--he was good at all; and though never seeking a quarrel, he would not put up with the slightest insult. He killed three Frenchmen in Paris, in quarrels forced upon him. I remember, in October, 1815, being asked by a friend to dine at Beauvillier's, in the Rue Richelieu, when Sir Charles S--, who was well known to us, occupied a table at the farther end of the room. About the middle of the dinner we heard a most extraordinary noise, and, on looking up, perceived that it arose from S--'s table; he was engaged in beating the head of a smartly-dressed gentleman with one of the long French loaves so well known to all who have visited France. Upon asking the reason of such rough treatment on the part of our countryman, he said he would serve all Frenchmen in the same manner if they insulted him. The offence, it seems, proceeded from the person who had just been chastised in so summary a manner: he had stared and laughed at S-- in a rude way, for having ordered three bottles of wine to be placed upon his table. The upshot of all this was a duel, which took place next day at a place near Vincennes, and in which S-- shot the unfortunate jester.

When Sir Charles returned to Valenciennes, where he commanded the Engineers, he found on his arrival a French officer waiting to avenge the death of his relation, who had only been shot ten days before at Vincennes. They accordingly fought, before S-- had time even to shave himself or eat his breakfast; he having only just arrived in his coupe from Paris. The meeting took place in the fosse of the fortress, and the first shot from S--'s pistol killed the French officer, who had actually travelled in the diligence from Paris for the purpose, as he boasted to his fellow-travellers, of killing an Englishman.

I recollect dining, in 1816, at Hervey Aston's, at the Hotel Breteuil in the Rue de Rivoli, opposite the Tuileries, where I met Seymour Bathurst and Captain E--, of the Artillery, a very good-looking man. After dinner, Mrs. Aston took us as far as Tortoni's, on her way to the Opera. On entering the cafe, Captain E-- did not touch his hat according to the custom of the country, but behaved himself, a la

John Bull, in a noisy and swaggering manner; upon which, General, then Colonel J--, went up to E-- and knocked off his hat, telling him that he hoped he would in future behave himself better. Aston, Bathurst, and I, waited for some time, expecting to see E-- knock J-- down, or, at all events, give him his card as a preliminary to a hostile meeting, on receiving such an insult; but he did nothing. We were very much disgusted and annoyed at a countryman's behaving in such a manner, and, after a meeting at my lodgings, we recommended Captain E--, in the strongest terms, to call out Colonel J--, but he positively refused to do so, as he said it was against his principles. This specimen of the white feather astonished us beyond measure. Captain E-- shortly after received orders to start for India, where I believe he died of cholera--in all probability of FUNK.

I do not think that Colonel J-- would altogether have escaped with impunity, after such a gratuitous insult to an English officer; but he retired into the country almost immediately after the incident at Tortoni's, and could not be found.

There were many men in our army who did not thus disgrace the British uniform when insulted by the French. I cannot omit the names of my old friends Captain Burges, Mike Fitzgerald, Charles Hesse, and Thoroton; each of whom, by their willingness to resent gratuitous offences, showed that insults to Englishmen were not to be committed with impunity. The last named officer having been grossly insulted by Marshal V--, without giving him the slightest provocation, knocked him down: this circumstance caused a great sensation in Paris, and brought about a court of inquiry, which ended in the acquittal of Captain Thoroton. My friend, B--, though he had only one leg, was a good swordsman, and contrived to kill a man at Lyons who had jeered him about the loss of his limb at Waterloo. My old and esteemed friend, Mike Fitzgerald, son of Lord Edward and the celebrated Pamela, was always ready to measure swords with the Frenchmen; and, after a brawl at Silves', the then fashionable Bonapartist cafe at the corner of the Rue Lafitte and the Boulevard, in which two of our Scotch countrymen showed the white feather, he and another officer placed their own cards over the chimney-piece in the principal room of the cafe, offering to fight any man, or number of men, for the frequent public insult offered to Britons. This challenge, however, was never answered.

A curious duel took place at Beauvais during the occupation of France by our army. A Captain B--, of one of our cavalry regiments quartered in that town, was insulted by a French officer, B-- demanded satisfaction, which was accepted; but the Frenchman would not fight with pistols. B-- would not fight with swords; so at last it was agreed that they should fight on horseback, with lances. The duel took place in the neighbourhood of Beauvais, and a crowd assembled to witness it. B-- received three wounds; but, by a lucky prod, eventually killed his man. B-- was a fine-looking man and a good horseman. My late friend the Baron de P--, so well known in Parisian circles, was second to the Frenchman on this occasion.

A friend of mine--certainly not of a quarrelsome turn, but considered by his friends, on the contrary, as rather a good-natured man--had three duels forced upon him in the course of a few weeks. He had formed a liaison with a person whose extraordinary beauty got him into several scrapes and disputes. In January 1 1817, a few days after this acquaintance had been formed, Jack B--, well known at that time in the best society in London, became madly in love with the fair lady, and attempted one night to enter her private box at Drury Lane; this my friend endeavoured to prevent; violent language was used, and a duel was the consequence. The parties met a few miles from London, in a field close to the Uxbridge Road, where B--, who was a hot-tempered man, did his best to kill my friend; but, after the exchange of two shots, without injury to either party, they were separated by their seconds. B-- was the son of Lady Bridget B--, and the seconds were Payne, uncle to George Payne, and Colonel Joddrell of the Guards.

Soon after this incident, my friend accompanied the lady to Paris, where they took up their residence at Meurice's, in the Rue de l'Echiquier. The day after their arrival, they went out to take a walk in the Palais Royal, and were followed by a half-pay officer of Napoleon's army, Colonel D.--a notorious duellist, who observed to the people about him that he was going to bully "un Anglais." This man was exceedingly rude in his remarks, uttered in a loud voice; and after every sort of insult expressed in words, he had the impudence to put his arm round the lady's waist. My friend indignantly asked the colonel what he meant; upon which the ruffian spat in my friend's face: but he did not get off with impunity, for my friend, who had a crab stick in his hand, caught him a blow on the side of the head, which dropped him. The Frenchman jumped up, and rushed at the Englishman; but they were separated by the bystanders. Cards were exchanged, and a meeting was arranged to take place the next morning in the neighbourhood of Passy. When my friend, accompanied by his second, Captain H--, of the 18th, came upon the ground, he found the colonel boasting of the number of officers of all nations whom he had killed, and saying, "I'll now complete my list by killing an Englishman." "Mon petit tir aura bientot ton conte, car je tire fort bien." My friend quietly said, "Je ne tire pas mal non plus," and took his place. The colonel, who seems to have been a horrible ruffian, after a good deal more swaggering and bravado, placed himself opposite, and, on the signal being given, the colonel's ball went through my friend's whiskers, whilst his ball pierced his adversary's heart, who fell dead without a groan.

This duel made much noise in Paris, and the survivor left immediately for Chantilly, where he passed some time. On his return to Paris, the second of the man who had been killed, Commander P., insulted and challenged my friend. A meeting was accordingly agreed upon, and pistols were again the weapons used. Again my friend won the toss, and told his second, Captain H--, that he would not kill his antagonist, though he richly deserved death for wishing to take the life of a person who had never offended him; but that he would give him a lesson which he should remember. My friend accordingly shot his antagonist in the knee; and I remember to have seen him limping about the streets of Paris twenty years after this event.

When the result of this second duel was known, not less than eleven challenges from Bonapartists were received by the gentleman in question; but any further encounters were put a stop to by the Minister of War, or the Duc d'Angouleme (I forget which), who threatened to place the officers under arrest if they followed up this quarrel any further. When the news reached England, the Duke of York said that my friend could not have acted otherwise than he had done in the first duel, considering the gross provocation that he had received; but he thought it would have been better if the second duel had been avoided.

In the deeds I have narrated, the English seem to have had the advantage, but many others took place, in which Englishmen were killed or wounded: these I have not mentioned, as their details do not recur to my memory; but I do not remember a single occasion on which Frenchmen were not the aggressors. At a somewhat later period than this, the present Marquis of H--, then Lord B--, had a duel with the son of the Bonapartist General L--. General S-- was Lord B--'s second, and the principals exchanged several shots without injury to either party. This duel, like the preceding, originated with the Frenchman, who insulted the Englishman at the Theatre Francais in the most unprovoked manner. At the present day our fiery neighbours are much more amenable to reason, and if you are but civil, they will be civil to you; duels consequently are of rare occurrence. Let us hope that the frequency and the animus displayed in these hostile meetings originated in national wounded vanity rather than in personal animosity.

In the autumn of 1821 I was living in Paris, when my old friend H--, Adjutant of the 1st Foot Guards, called upon me, and requested that I would be his second in a duel with Mr. N--, an officer in the same regiment. After hearing what he had to say, and thinking I could serve him, I consented. It was agreed by Captain F--, R.N., of Pitmore, Mr. N--'s second, that the duel should take place in the Bois de Boulogne. After an exchange of shots, Captain F. and myself put an end to the duel. The cause of the quarrel was that Mr. N--, now Lord G--, proclaimed in the presence of Captain H-- and other officers, that a lady, the wife of a brother officer, was "what she ought not to be." When the report reached the ear of the Colonel, H. R. H. the Duke of York requested Mr. N-- to leave the regiment, or be brought to a court-martial; and then the duel took place, happily without bloodshed. Both of the officers, it need scarcely be stated, behaved with courage and coolness.

PISTOL SHOOTING

From 1820 to 1830 pistol shooting was not much practised. One evening, in the Salon des Etrangers, I was introduced to General F--, a very great duellist, and the terror of every regiment he commanded; he was considered by Napoleon to be one of his best cavalry officers, but was never in favour, in consequence of his duelling propensities. It was currently reported that F--, in a duel with a very young officer lost his toss, and his antagonist fired first at him; when, finding he had not been touched, he deliberately walked close up to the young man, saying, "Je plains ta mere," and shot him dead. But there were some doubts of the truth of this story; and I trust, for the honour of humanity, that it was either an invention or a gross exaggeration.

The night I was introduced to F--, I was told to be on my guard, as he was a dangerous character. He was very fond of practising with pistols, and I frequently met him at Lapage's, the only place at that time where gentlemen used to shoot. F--, in the year 1822, was very corpulent, and wore an enormous cravat, in order, it was said, to hide two scars received in battle. He was a very slow shot.

The famous Junot, Governor-General of Paris, whom I never saw, was considered to be the best shot in France. My quick shooting surprised the habitues at Lapage's, where we fired at a spot chalked on the figure of a Cossack painted on a board, and by word of command, "One--two--three." F--, upon my firing and hitting the mark forty times in succession, at the distance of twenty paces, shrieked out, "Tonnerre de Dieu, c'est magnifique!" We were ever afterwards on good terms, and supped frequently together at the Salon. At Manton's, on one occasion, I hit the wafer nineteen times out of twenty. When my battalion was on duty at the Tower in 1819, it happened to be very cold, and much snow covered the parade and trees. For our amusement it was proposed to shoot at the sparrows in the trees from Lady Jane Grey's room; and it fell to my lot to bag eleven, without missing one: this, I may say, without flattering myself, was considered the best pistol-shooting ever heard of.

Manton assigned as the reason why pistols had become the usual arms for duels, the story (now universally laughed at) of Sheridan and Captain Matthews fighting with swords on the ground, and mangling each other in a frightful way. These combatants narrated their own story; but its enormous exaggeration has been proved even on Sheridan's own evidence, and the blood that poured from him seems merely to have been the excellent claret of the previous night's debauch. The number of wounds said to have been inflicted on each other was something so incredible that nothing but the solemn asseverations of the parties could have gained belief; and in those days Sheridan had not obtained that reputation for rodomontade which he afterwards enjoyed by universal consent.

THE FAUBOURG ST. GERMAIN

The distinguishing characteristics of the residents of the "noble Faubourg," as it was called at the time I am speaking of, were indomitable pride and exclusiveness, with a narrow-minded ignorance of all beyond the circle in which its members moved. In our day of comparative equality and general civility, no one who has not arrived at my age, and lived in Paris, can form any idea of the insolence and hauteur of the higher classes of society in 1815. The glance of unutterable disdain which the painted old duchesse of the Restoration cast upon the youthful belles of the Chausse d'Antin, or the handsome widows of Napoleon's army of heroes, defies description. Although often responded to by a sarcastic sneer at the antediluvian charms of the emigree, yet the look of contempt and disgust often sank deep into the victim's heart, leaving there germs which showed themselves fifteen years later in the revolution of 1830. In those days, this privileged class was surrounded by a charmed circle, which no one could by any means break through. Neither personal attractions nor mental qualifications formed a passport into that exclusive society; to enter which the small nobility of the provinces, or the nouveau riche, sighed in vain. It would have been easier for a young Guardsman to make his way into the Convent des Oiseaux--the fashionable convent in Paris--than for any of these parvenus to force an entrance into the Faubourg St. Germain.

One of the first acts which followed the Restoration of the Bourbons was the grant of a pecuniary indemnity, amounting to a milliard, or forty millions sterling, to be distributed amongst the emigres who had lost fortunes or estates by their devotion to the royal family. They had now, therefore, the means of receiving their friends, political partisans, and foreigners, with more than usual splendour; and it must be admitted that those who were thought worthy to be received were treated like spoiled children, and petted and flattered to their heart's content. In their own houses they were really des grands seigneurs, and quite incapable of treating their invited guests with the insolence that became the fashion among the Jewish parvenus during the reign of the "citizen king." It is one thing to disdain those whom one does not think worthy of our acquaintance, and another to insult those whom one has thought proper to invite.

In their own houses, the inhabitants of the Faubourg St. Germain were scrupulously polite: even if some enterprising foreigner should have got in surreptitiously, as long as he was under his host's roof he was treated with perfect courtesy; though ignominiously "cut" for the remainder of his days. All this was not very amiable; but the inhabitants of the "noble Faubourg" were never distinguished for their amiability. Their best characteristics were the undaunted courage with which they met death upon the scaffold, and the cheerfulness and resignation with which they ate the bitter bread of exile. In general, les grandes dames were not remarkable for their personal attractions, nor for the elegance of their appearance or dress. The galaxy of handsome women that formed the court of the Emperor had perhaps sent beauty somewhat out of fashion; for the high-born ladies who took their place were what we should call dowdy, and had nothing distinguished in their appearance. Many of those who belonged to the most ancient families were almost vulgar in outward form and feature: their manner had a peculiar off-hand, easy style; and they particularly excelled in setting down any unlucky person who had happened to offend them. Their main object, at this time, was to stand well at court, therefore they adapted themselves to circumstances, and could be devout with the Dauphine and sceptical with Louis the Eighteenth.

The men of the aristocracy of the Revolution were less clever and satirical than the women; but, on the other hand, they had far more of the distinguished bearing and graceful urbanity of the grands seigneurs of the olden time. The emigre nobles would have gazed with unutterable horror at their degenerate descendants of the present day; but these young, booted, bearded, cigar-smoking scions of la jeune France would have run round their courteous, but, perhaps, rather slow ancestors, in all the details of daily life.

The principal houses of reception in those days were those of the Montmorencys, the Richelieus, Birons, Rohans, Goutaut Talleyrands, Beauffremonts, Luxemburgs, Crillons, Choiseuls, Chabots, Fitzjames, Grammonts, Latours de Pin, Coislins, and Maillys. Most of these mansions are now occupied as public offices, or Jesuitical schools, or by foreign Ministers. Those who are now supposed to be the great people of the Faubourg St. Germain are nothing more than actors, who put on a motley dress and appear before the public with the view of attracting that attention to which they are not entitled; it is, therefore, an error to suppose that the modern faubourg is anything like what it was during the days of the Bourbons. At the present moment the only practical aid the inhabitants of this locality can accord to the legitimist cause in Europe, is by getting up subscriptions for the Papacy, and such exiled Sovereigns as Francis II.; and, in order to do so, they generally address themselves to married women and widows: in fact, it is from the purses of susceptible females, many of whom are English, that donations are obtained for legitimacy and Popery in distress.

It is to be regretted that the most renowned and ancient families of France have, in society and politics, yielded their places to another class. That refinement of perception, sensitiveness, and gentle bearing, which take three or four generations to produce, are no longer the characteristics of Parisian society. The gilded saloons of the Tuileries, and those magnificent hotels whose architects have not been geniuses of art, but the children of Mammon, are occupied by the Jew speculator, the political parasite, the clever schemer, and those who--whilst following the fortune of the great man who rules France--are nothing better than harpies. Most of these pretended devotees of imperialism have, speaking figuratively, their portmanteaus perpetually packed, ready for flight. The Emperor's good nature, as regards his entourage, has never allowed him to get rid of men who, perhaps, ought not to be seen so near the Imperial throne of France. The weakest feature of Napoleon III.'s Government is the conspicuous presence of a few persons in high places, whose cupidity is so extravagant that, in order to gratify their lust of wealth, they would not hesitate, indirectly at least, to risk a slur on the reputation of their master and benefactor, in order to gain their own ends.

THE SALON DES ETRANGERS IN PARIS

When the allies entered Paris, after the Battle of Waterloo, the English gentlemen sought, instinctively, something like a club. Paris, however, possessed nothing of the sort; but there was a much more dangerous establishment than the London clubs, namely, a rendezvous for confirmed gamblers. The Salon des Etrangers was most gorgeously furnished, provided with an excellent kitchen and wines, and was conducted by the celebrated Marquis de Livry, who received the guests and did the honours with a courtesy which made him famous throughout Europe. The Marquis presented an extraordinary likeness to the Prince Regent of England, who actually sent Lord Fife over to Paris to ascertain this momentous fact. The play which took place in these saloons was frequently of the most reckless character; large fortunes were often lost, the losers disappearing, never more to be heard of. Amongst the English habitues were the Hon. George T--, the late Henry Baring, Lord Thanet, Tom Sowerby, Cuthbert, Mr. Steer, Henry Broadwood, and Bob Arnold.

The Hon. George T--, who used to arrive from London with a very considerable letter of credit expressly to try his luck at the Salon des Etrangers, at length contrived to lose his last shilling at rouge et noir. When he had lost everything he possessed in the world, he got up and exclaimed, in an excited manner, "If I had Canova's Venus and Adonis from Alton Towers, my uncle's country seat, it should be placed on the rouge, for black has won fourteen times running!"

The late Henry Baring was more fortunate at hazard than his countryman, but his love of gambling was the cause of his being excluded from the banking establishment. Col. Sowerby, of the Guards, was one of the most inveterate players in Paris; and, as is frequently the case with a fair player, a considerable loser. But, perhaps, the most incurable gamester amongst the English was Lord Thanet, whose income was not less than 50,000L. a year, every farthing of which he lost at play. Cuthbert dissipated the whole of his fortune in like manner. In fact, I do not remember any instance where those who spent their time in this den did not lose all they possessed.

The Marquis de L-- had a charming villa at Romainville, near Paris, to which, on Sundays, he invited not only those gentlemen who were the most prodigal patrons of his salon, but a number of ladies, who were dancers and singers conspicuous at the opera; forming a society of the strangest character, the male portion of which were bent on losing their money, whilst the ladies were determined to get rid of whatever virtue they might still have left. The dinners on these occasions were supplied by the chef of the Salon des Etrangers, and were such as few renommes of the kitchens of France could place upon the table.

Amongst the constant guests was Lord Fife, the intimate friend of George IV., with Mdlle. Noblet, a danseuse, who gave so much satisfaction to the habitues of the pit at the opera, both in Paris and London. His lordship spent a fortune upon her; his presents in jewels, furniture, articles of dress, and money, exceeded 40,000L. In return for all this generosity, Lord Fife asked nothing more than the lady's flattery and professions of affection.

Hall Standish was always to be seen in this circle; and his own hotel in the Rue le Pelletier was often lighted up, and fetes given to the theatrical and demi-monde. Standish died in Spain, leaving his gallery of pictures to Louis Philippe.

Amongst others who visited the Salon des Etrangers were Sir Francis Vincent, Gooch, Green, Ball Hughes, and many others whose names I no longer remember. Of foreigners the most conspicuous were Blucher, General Ormano, father-in-law of Count Walewski, Pacto, and Clari, as well as most of the ambassadors at the court of the Tuileries. As at Crockford's, a magnificent supper was provided every night for all who thought proper to avail themselves of it. The games principally played were rouge et noir and hazard; the former producing an immense profit, for not only were the whole of the expenses of this costly establishment defrayed by the winnings of the bank, but a very large sum was paid annually to the municipality of Paris. I recollect a young Irishman, Mr. Gough, losing a large fortune at this tapis vert. After returning home about two A.M., he sat down and wrote a letter, giving reasons as to why he was about to commit suicide: these, it is needless to say, were simply his gambling reverses. A pistol shot through the brain terminated his existence. Sir Francis Vincent--a man of old family and considerable fortune--was another victim of this French hell, who contrived to get rid of his magnificent property, and then disappeared from society.

In calling up my recollections of the Salon des Etrangers, some forty years since, I see before me the noble form and face of the Hungarian Count Hunyady, the chief gambler of the day, who created considerable sensation in his time. He became tres a la mode: his horses, carriage, and house were considered perfect, while his good looks were the theme of universal admiration. There were ladies' cloaks "a la Huniade," whilst the illustrious Borel, of the Rocher de Cancaile, named new dishes after the famous Hungarian. Hunyady's luck for a long time was prodigious: no bank could resist his attacks; and at one time he must have been a winner of nearly two millions of francs. His manners were particularly calm and gentlemanlike; he sat apparently unmoved, with his right hand in the breast of his coat, whilst thousands depended upon the turning of a card or the hazard of a die. His valet, however, confided to some indiscreet friend that his nerves were not of such iron temper as he would have made people believe, and that the count bore in the morning the bloody marks of his nails, which he had pressed into his chest in the agony of an unsuccessful turn of fortune. The streets of Paris were at that time not very safe; consequently the Count was usually attended to his residence by two gensdarmes, in order to prevent his being attacked by robbers. Hunyady was not wise enough (what gamblers are?) to leave Paris with his large winnings, but continued as usual to play day and night. A run of bad luck set in against him, and he lost not only the whole of the money he had won, but a very large portion of his own fortune. He actually borrowed 50L. of the well-known Tommy Garth--who was himself generally more in the borrowing than the lending line--to take him back to Hungary.

THE DUCHESS DE BERRI AT MASS AT THE CHAPELLE ROYALE

I had the honour of being invited to an evening party at the Tuileries in the winter of 1816, and was in conversation with the Countess de l'Espinasse, when the Duchess did me the honour to ask me if I intended going to St. Germain to hunt. I replied in the negative, not having received an invitation; upon which the Duchess graciously observed that if I would attend mass the following morning in the Royal Chapel, she would manage it. Accordingly I presented myself there dressed in a black coat and trousers and white neckcloth; but at the entrance, a huge Swiss told me I could not enter the chapel without knee-buckles. At that moment Alexandre Gerardin, the grand veneur, came to my assistance; he spoke to the Duchess, who immediately gave instructions that Mr. Gronow was to be admitted "sans culottes." The card for the hunt came; but the time to get the uniform was so short, that I was prevented going to St. Germain. At that time the fascinating Duchess de Berri was the theme of admiration of everyone. All who could obtain admission to the chapelle were charmed with the grace with which, on passing through the happy group who had been fortunate enough to gain the privilege, she cast her glance of recognition upon those who were honoured with her notice. When again I had the honour of being in the presence of the Duchess, she inquired whether the hunt amused me; and upon my telling her that I had been unable to go, in consequence of the want of the required uniform, the Duchess archly remarked "Ah! M. le Capitaine, parceque vous n'avez pas jamais des culottes."

LORD WESTMORELAND

When I was presented at the Court of Louis XVIII., Lord Westmoreland, the grandfather of the present lord, accompanied Sir Charles Stewart to the Tuileries. On our arrival in the room where the King was, we formed ourselves into a circle, when the King good-naturedly inquired after Lady Westmoreland, from whom his lordship was divorced, and whether she was in Paris. Upon this, the noble lord looked sullen, and refused to reply to the question put by the King. His Majesty, however, repeated it, when Lord Westmoreland hallooed out, in bad French, "Je ne sais pas, je ne sais pas, je ne sais pas." Louis, rising, said, "Assez, milord; assez, milord."

On one occasion, Lord Westmoreland, who was Lord Privy Seal, being asked what office he held, replied, "Le Chancelier est le grand sceau (Sot); moi je suis le petit sceau d' Angleterre." On another occasion, he wished to say "I would if I could, but I can't," and rendered it, "Je voudrais si je coudrais, mais je ne cannais pas."

ALDERMAN WOOD

Among the many English who then visited Paris was Alderman Wood, who had previously filled the office of Lord Mayor of London. He ordered a hundred visiting cards, inscribing upon them, "Alderman Wood, feu Lord Maire de Londres," which he had largely distributed amongst people of rank--having translated the word "late" into "feu," which I need hardly state means "dead."

THE OPERA

A few years after the restoration of the Bourbons, the opera was the grand resort of all the fashionable world. Sostennes de la Rochefoucauld was Minister of the Household, and his office placed him at the head of all the theatres. M. de la Rochefoucauld was exceedingly polite to our countrymen, and gave permission to most of our dandies to go behind the scenes, where Bigottini, Fanny Bias, Vestris, Anatole, Paul, Albert, and the other principal dancers, congregated. One of our countrymen, having been introduced by M. de la Rochefoucauld to Mademoiselle Bigottini, the beautiful and graceful dancer, in the course of conversation with this gentleman, asked him in what part of the theatre he was placed; upon which he replied, "Mademoiselle, dans un loge rotie," instead of "grillee." The lady could not understand what he meant, until his introducer explained the mistake, observing, "Les diables des Anglais pensent toujours a leur Rosbif."

FANNY ELSSLER

In 1822 I saw this beautiful person for the first time. She was originally one of the figurantes at the opera at Vienna, and was at this time about fourteen years of age, and of delicate and graceful proportions. Her hair was auburn, her eyes blue and large, and her face wore an expression of great tenderness. Some years after the

Duke of Reichstadt, the son of the great Napoleon, was captivated with her beauty; in a word, he became her acknowledged admirer, while her marvellous acting and dancing drew around her all the great men of the German court. The year following she went to Naples, where a brother of the King fell desperately in love with her. Mademoiselle Elssler went soon afterwards to Paris, where her wit electrified all the fashionable world, and her dancing and acting in the Diable Boiteux made the fortune of the entrepreneur. In London her success was not so striking; but her cachucha will long be remembered, as one of the most exquisite exhibitions of female grace and power ever seen at her Majesty's Theatre, and in expressiveness, her pantomimic powers were unrivalled.

CHARLES X. AND LOUIS PHILIPPE

When the father of the present ex-King of Naples came to Paris during the reign of Charles X., Louis Philippe, then Duke of Orleans, living at the Palais Royal, gave a very grand fete to his royal cousin. I had the honour to be one of the party invited, and witnessed an extraordinary scene, which I think worth relating. About eleven o'clock, when the rooms were crowded, Charles X. arrived, with a numerous suite. On entering, he let fall his pocket-handkerchief--it was then supposed by accident; upon this, Louis Philippe fell upon one knee and presented the handkerchief to his Sovereign; who smiled and said, "Merci, mon cher; merci." This incident was commented upon for many days, and several persons said that the handkerchief was purposely thrown down to see whether Louis Philippe would pick it up.

At that period, the Orleans family were en mauvais odeur at the Tuileries, and consequently, this little incident created considerable gossip among the courtly quidnuncs. I remember that when Lord William Bentinck was asked what he thought of the circumstance, he good-naturedly answered, "The King most probably wanted to know how the wind blew."

It was known that a large number of persons hostile to the court were invited; and among these were Casimir Perier, the Dupins, Lafitte, Benjamin Constant, and a host of others who a few years afterwards drove out the eldest branch that occupied the throne to make way for Louis Philippe.

LORD THANET

The late Lord Thanet, celebrated for having been imprisoned in the Tower for his supposed predilection for republicanism, passed much of his time in Paris, particularly at the Salon des Etrangers. His lordship's infatuation for play was such, that when the gambling-tables were closed, he invited those who remained to play at chicken-hazard and ecarte; the consequence was that, one night, he left off a loser of 120,000L. When told of his folly and the probability of his having been cheated, he exclaimed, "Then I consider myself lucky in not having lost twice that sum!"

LORD GRANVILLE, THE BRITISH AMBASSADOR

Soon after Lord Granville's appointment, a strange occurrence took place at one of the public gambling-houses. A colonel, on half-pay, in the British service, having lost every farthing that he possessed, determined to destroy himself, together with all those who were instrumental in his ruin. Accordingly, he placed a canister full of fulminating powder under the table, and set it on fire: it blew up, but fortunately no one was hurt. The police arrested the colonel, and placed him in prison; he was, however, through the humane interposition of our ambassador, sent out of France as a madman.

MARSHAL BLUCHER

Marshal Blucher, though a very fine fellow, was a very rough diamond, with the manners of a common soldier. On his arrival in Paris, he went every day to the salon, and played the highest stakes at rouge et noir. The salon, during the time that the marshal remained in Paris, was crowded by persons who came to see him play. His manner of playing was anything but gentlemanlike, and when he lost, he used to swear in German at everything that was French, looking daggers at the croupiers.

He generally managed to lose all he had about him, also all the money his servant, who was waiting in the ante-chamber, carried. I recollect looking attentively at the manner in which he played; he would put his right hand into his pocket, and bring out several rouleaus of Napoleons, and throw them on the red or black. If he won the first coup, he would allow it to remain; but when the croupier stated that the table was not responsible for more than ten thousand francs, then Blucher would roar like a lion, and rap out oaths in his native language, which would doubtless have met with great success at Billingsgate, if duly translated: fortunately, they were not heeded, as they were not understood by the lookers-on.

At that period there were rumours--and reliable ones, too--that Blucher and the Duke of Wellington were at loggerheads. The Prussians wanted to blow up the Bridge of Jena; but the Duke sent a battalion of our regiment to prevent it, and the Prussian engineers who were mining the bridge were civilly sent away: this circumstance created some ill-will between the chiefs.

A sort of congress of the Emperors of Austria and Russia and the King of Prussia, with Blucher and Wellington, met at the Hotel of Foreign Affairs, on the Boulevard, when, after much ado, the Duke of Wellington emphatically declared that if any of the monuments were destroyed he would take the British army from Paris: this threat had the desired effect. Nevertheless, Blucher levied contributions on the poor Parisians, and his army was newly clothed. The Bank of France was called upon to furnish him with several thousand pounds, which, it was said, were to reimburse him for the money lost at play. This, with many other instances of extortion and tyranny, was the cause of Blucher's removal, and he took his departure by order of the King.

I once saw a regiment of Prussians march down the Rue St. Honore when a line of half-a-dozen hackney-coachmen were quietly endeavouring to make their way in a contrary direction; suddenly some of the Prussian soldiers left their ranks, and with the butt-end of their muskets knocked the poor coachmen off their seats. I was in uniform, and felt naturally ashamed at what I had seen: some Frenchmen came up to me and requested me to report what I had witnessed to the Duke of Wellington; but, upon my telling them it would be of no avail, they one and all said the English ought to blush at having allies and friends capable of such wanton brutality.

The fact is that the French had behaved so ill at Berlin, after the Battle of Jena, in 1806, that the Prussians had sworn to be revenged, if ever they had the opportunity to visit upon France the cruelties, the extortion, insults, and hard usage their own capital had suffered; and they kept their word.

One afternoon, when upwards of a hundred Prussian officers entered the galleries of the Palais Royal, they visited all the shops in turn, insulting the women and striking the men, breaking the windows and turning everything upside down: nothing, indeed, could have been more outrageous than their conduct. When information was brought to Lord James Hay of what was going on, he went out, and arrived just as a troop of French gensdarmes were on the point of charging the Prussians, then in the garden. He lost no time in calling out his men, and, placing himself between the gensdarmes and the officers, said he should fire upon the first who moved. The Prussians then came to him and said, "We had all vowed to return upon the heads of the French in Paris the insults that they had heaped upon our countrymen in Berlin; we have kept our vow, and we will now retire." Nothing could equal the bitter hatred which existed, and still exists, between the French and the Prussians.

JEW MONEY-LENDERS

One of the features of high society after the long war was a passion for gambling; so universal was it that there are few families of distinction who do not even to the present day retain unpleasant reminiscences of the period. When people become systematic players, they are often obliged to raise money at an exorbitant interest, and usually under such circumstances fly to the Israelites. I have often heard players wish these people in almost every uncomfortable quarter of the known and unknown worlds. The mildness and civility with which the Christian in difficulties always addresses the moneyed Israelite, contrast forcibly with the opprobrious epithets lavished on him when the day for settlement comes. When a man requires money to pay his debts of honour, and borrows from the Jews, he knows perfectly well what he is doing; though one of the last things which foolish people learn is how to trace their own errors to their proper source. Hebrew money-lenders could not thrive if there were no borrowers: the gambler brings about his own ruin. The characteristics of the Jew are never more perceptible than when they come in contact with gentlemen to ruin them. On such occasions, the Jew is humble, supercilious, blunderingly flattering; and if he can become the agent of any dirty work, is only too happy to be so, in preference to a straightforward and honest transaction. No man is more vulgarly insulting to those dependent upon him than the Jew, who invariably cringes to his superiors; above all, he is not a brave man. It will be seen, from these observations, what is my opinion of a class of traders who in all parts of the world are sure to embrace what may be termed illicit and illegitimate commerce. At the same time, I suspect that the Jew simply avails himself of the weakness and vices of mankind, and will continue in this line of business so long as imprudent and extravagant humanity remains what it is.

Two usurers, who obtained much notoriety from the high game which was brought to them, were men known by the names of Jew King and Solomon. These were of very different characters: King was a man of some talent, and had good taste in the fine arts. He had made the peerage a complete study, knew the exact position of everyone who was connected with a coronet, the value of their property, how deeply the estates were mortgaged, and what encumbrances weighed upon them. Nor did his knowledge stop there: by dint of sundry kind attentions to the clerks of the leading banking-houses, he was aware of the balances they kept; and the credit attached to their names; so that, to the surprise of the borrower, he let him into the secrets of his own actual position. He gave excellent dinners, at which many of the highest personages of the realm were present; and when they fancied that they were about to meet individuals whom it would be upon their conscience to recognize elsewhere, were not a little amused to find clients quite as highly placed as themselves, and with purses quite as empty. King had a well-appointed house in Clarges Street; but it was in a villa upon the banks of the Thames, which had been beautifully fitted up by Walsh Porter in the Oriental style, and which I believe is now the seat of one of the most favoured votaries of the Muses, Sir Edward Bulwer Lytton, that his hospitalities were most lavishly and luxuriously exercised. Here it was that Sheridan told his host that he liked his table better than his multiplication table; to which his host, who was not only witty, but often the cause of wit in others, replied, "I know, Mr. Sheridan: your taste is more for Jo-king than for Jew

King," alluding to King, the actor's admirable performance in Sheridan's School for Scandal.

King kept a princely establishment, and a splendid equipage which he made to serve as an advertisement of his calling. A yellow carriage, with panels emblazoned with a well-executed shield and armorial bearings, and drawn by two richly-caparisoned steeds, the Jehu on the box wearing, according to the fashion of those days, a coat of many capes, a powdered wig, and gloves a l'Henri Quatre, and two spruce footmen in striking but not gaudy livery, with long canes in their hands, daily made its appearance in the Park from four to seven in the height of the season. Mrs. King was a fine-looking woman, and being dressed in the height of fashion, she attracted innumerable gazers, who pronounced the whole turn-out to be a work of refined taste, and worthy a man of "so much principal and interest."

It happened that during one of these drives, Lord William L., a man of fashion, but, like other of the great men of the day, an issuer of paper money discounted at high rates by the usurers, was thrown off his horse. Mr. and Mrs. King immediately quitted the carriage and placed the noble lord within. On this circumstance being mentioned in the clubs, Brummell observed it was only "a Bill Jewly (duly) taken up and honoured."

Solomon indulged in many aliases, being known by the names of Goldsched, Slowman, as well as by other noms de guerre; and he was altogether of a different cast from King, being avaricious, distrustful, and difficult to deal with. He counted upon his gains with all the grasping feverishness of the miser; and owing to his great caution he had an immense command of money, which the confidence of his brethren placed in his hands. To the jewellers, the coachmakers, and the tailors, who were obliged to give exorbitant accommodation to their aristocratic customers, and were eventually paid in bills of an incredibly long date, Solomon was of inestimable use. Hamlet, Houlditch, and other dependants upon the nobility, were often compelled to seek his assistance.

Hamlet, the jeweller, was once looked up to as the richest tradesman at the West End. His shop at the corner of Cranbourne Alley exhibited a profuse display of gold and silver plate, whilst in the jewel room sparkled diamonds, amethysts, rubies, and other precious stones, in every variety of setting. He was constantly called on to advance money upon such objects, which were left in pawn only to be taken out on the occasion of a great banquet, or when a court dress was to be worn. His gains were enormous, though it was necessary to give long credit; and his bills for twenty or thirty thousand pounds were eagerly discounted. In fact, he was looked upon as a second Croesus, or a Crassus, who could have bought the Roman empire; and his daughter's hand was sought in marriage by peers. But all at once the mighty bubble collapsed. He had advanced money to the Duke of York, and had received as security property in Nova Scotia, consisting chiefly of mines, which, when he began to work them, turned out valueless, after entailing enormous expense. Loss upon loss succeeded, and in the end bankruptcy. I have even heard that this man, once so envied for his wealth, died the inmate of an almshouse.

Some persons of rank, tempted by the offers of these usurers, lent their money to them at a very high interest. A lady of some position lent a thousand pounds to King, on the promise of receiving annually 15 per cent.; which he continued to pay with the utmost regularity. Her son being in want of money applied for a loan of a thousand pounds, which King granted at the rate of 80 per cent.; lending him of course his mother's money. In a moment of tenderness the young man told his tale to her, when she immediately went to King and upbraided him for not making her a party to his gains, and demanded her money back. King refused to return it, saying that he had never engaged to return the principal; and dared her to take any proceedings against him, as, being a married woman, she had no power over the money. She, however, acknowledged it to her husband, obtained his forgiveness, and after threats of legal interference, King was compelled to refund the money, besides losing much of his credit and popularity by the transaction.

LORD ALVANLEY

To Lord Alvanley was awarded the reputation, good or bad, of all the witticisms in the clubs after the abdication of the throne of dandyism by Brummell; who, before that time, was always quoted as the sayer of good things, as Sheridan had been some time before. Lord Alvanley had the talk of the day completely under his control, and was the arbiter of the school for scandal in St. James's. A bon mot attributed to him gave rise to the belief that Solomon caused the downfall and disappearance of Brummell; for on some friends of the prince of dandies observing that if he had remained in London something might have been done for him by his old associates, Alvanley replied, "He has done quite right to be off: it was Solomon's judgment."

When Sir Lumley Skeffington, who had been a lion in his day--and whose spectacle, the Sleeping Beauty, produced at a great expense on the stage, had made him looked up to as deserving all the blandishments of fashionable life--re-appeared some years after his complete downfall and seclusion in the bench, he fancied that by a very gay external appearance he would recover his lost position; but he found his old friends very shy of him. Alvanley being asked, on one occasion, who that smart-looking individual was, answered, "It is a second edition of the Sleeping Beauty bound in calf, richly gilt, and illustrated by many cuts."

One of the gay men of the day, named Judge, being incarcerated in the Bench, some one observed he believed it was the first instance of a Judge reaching the bench without being previously called to the bar; to which Alvanley replied, "Many a bad judge has been taken from the bench and placed at the bar." He used to say that Brummell was the only Dandelion that flourished year after year in the hot-bed of the fashionable world: he had taken root. Lions were generally annual, but Brummell was perennial, and quoted a letter from Walter Scott: "If you are celebrated for writing verses, or for slicing cucumbers, for being two feet taller, or two feet less, than any other biped, for acting plays when you should be whipped at school, or for attending schools and institutions when you should be preparing for your grave, your notoriety becomes a talisman, an 'open sesame,' which gives way to everything, till you are voted a bore, and discarded for a new plaything." This appeared in a letter from Walter Scott to the Earl of Dalkeith, when he himself, Belzoni, Master Betty the Roscius, and old Joseph Lancaster, the schoolmaster, were the lions of the season, and were one night brought together by my indefatigable old friend, Lady Cork, who was "the Lady of Lyons" of that day.

GENERAL PALMER

This excellent man had the last days of his life embittered by the money-lenders. He had commenced his career surrounded by every circumstance that could render existence agreeable; fortune, in his early days, having smiled most benignantly on him. His father was a man of considerable ability, and was to the past generation what Rowland Hill is in the present day--the great benefactor of correspondents. He first proposed and carried out the mail-coach system; and letters, instead of being at the mercy of postboys, and a private speculation in many instances, became the care of Government, and were transmitted under its immediate direction.

During the lifetime of Mr. Palmer, the reward due to him for his suggestions and his practical knowledge was denied; and he accordingly went to Bath, and became the manager and proprietor of the theatre, occasionally treading the boards himself, for which his elegant deportment and good taste eminently qualified him. He has often been mistaken for Gentleman Palmer, whose portrait is well drawn in the Memoir of Sheridan by Dr. Sigmond, prefixed to Bohn's edition of Sheridan's plays. Mr. Palmer was successful in his undertaking, and at his death, his son found himself the inheritor of a handsome fortune, and became a universal favourite in Bath.

The corporation of that city, consisting of thirty apothecaries, were, in those borough-mongering days, the sole electors to the House of Commons, and finding young Palmer hospitable, and intimate with the Marquis of Bath and Lord Camden, and likewise desiring for themselves and their families free access to the most agreeable theatre in England, returned him to Parliament. He entered the army and became a conspicuous officer in the 10th Hussars, which, being commanded by the Prince Regent, led him at once into Carlton House, the Pavilion at Brighton, and consequently into the highest society of the country; for which his agreeable manners, his amiable disposition, and his attainments, admirably qualified him. His fortune was sufficiently large for all his wants; but, unfortunately, as it turned out, the House of Commons voted to him, as the representative of his father, 100,000L., which he was desirous of laying out to advantage.

A fine opportunity, as he imagined, had presented itself to him; for, in travelling in the diligence from Lyons to Paris, a journey then requiring three days, he met a charming widow, who told a tale that had not only a wonderful effect upon his susceptible heart, but upon his amply-filled purse. She said her husband, who had been the proprietor of one of the finest estates in the neighbourhood of Bordeaux, was just dead, and that she was on her way to Paris to sell the property, that it might be divided, according to the laws of France, amongst the family. Owing, however, to the absolute necessity of forcing a sale, that which was worth an enormous sum would realize one-quarter only of its value. She described the property as one admirably fitted for the production of wine; that it was, in fact, the next estate to the Chateau Lafitte, and would prove a fortune to any capitalist. The fascinations of this lady, and the temptation of enormous gain to the speculator, impelled the gallant colonel to offer his services to relieve her from her embarrassment; and by the time the diligence arrived in Paris, he had become the proprietor of a fine domain, which was soon irrevocably fixed on him by the lady's notary, in return for a large sum of money: which, had the colonel proved a man of business, would no doubt have been amply repaid, and might have become the source of great wealth.

Palmer, however, conscious of his inability, looked around him for an active agent, and believed he had found one in a Mr. Gray, a man of captivating manners and good connexions, but almost as useless a person as the General himself. Fully confident in his own abilities, Gray had already been concerned in many speculations, not one of which had ever succeeded, but all had led to the demolition of large fortunes. Plausible in his address, and possessing many of those superficial qualities that please the multitude, he appeared to be able to secure for the claret--which was the production of the estate--a large clientele. Palmer's claret, under his auspices, began to be talked of in the clubs; and the bon vivant was anxious to secure a quantity of this highly-prized wine. The patronage of the Prince Regent was considered essential, who, with his egotistical good nature, and from a kindly feeling for Palmer, gave a dinner at Carlton House, when a fair trial was to be given to his claret. A select circle of gastronomes was to be present, amongst whom was Lord Yarmouth, well known in those days by the appellation of "Red-herrings," from his rubicund whiskers, hair, and face, and from the town of Yarmouth deriving its principal support from the importation from Holland of that fish; Sir Benjamin Bloomfield, Sir William Knighton, and Sir Thomas Tyrwhitt, were also of the party. The wine was produced, and was found excellent, and the spirits of the party ran high; the light wine animating them without intoxication. The Prince was delighted, and, as usual upon such occasions, told some of his best stories, quoted Shakspeare, and was particularly happy upon the bouquet of the wine as suited "to the holy Palmer's kiss."

Lord Yarmouth alone sat in moody silence, and, on being questioned as to the cause, replied that whenever he dined at his Royal Highness's table, he drank a claret which he much preferred--that which was furnished by Carbonell. The Prince immediately ordered a bottle of this wine; and to give them an opportunity of testing the difference, he desired that some anchovy sandwiches should be served up. Carbonell's wine was placed upon the table: it was a claret made expressly for the London market, well-dashed with Hermitage, and infinitely more to the taste of the Englishman than the delicately-flavoured wine they had been drinking. The banquet terminated in the Prince declaring his own wine superior to that of Palmer's, and suggesting that he should try some experiments on his estate to obtain a better wine. Palmer come from Carlton House much mortified. On Sir Thomas Tyrwhitt attempting to console him, and saying that it was the anchovies that had spoiled the taste of the connoisseurs, the general said loudly enough to be heard by Lord Yarmouth, "No; it was the confounded red herrings." A duel was very nearly the consequence.

General Palmer, feeling it his duty to follow the advice of the Prince, rooted out his old vines, planted new ones, tried all sorts of experiments at an immense cost, but with little or no result. He and his agent, in consequence, got themselves into all sorts of difficulties, mortgaged the property, borrowed largely, and were at last obliged to have recourse to usurers, to life assurances, and every sort of expedient to raise money. The theatre at Bath was sold, the Reform in Parliament robbed him of his seat, and at last he and his agent became ruined men. A subscription would have been raised to relieve him, but he preferred ending his days in poverty to living upon the bounty of his friends. He sold his commission, and was plunged in the deepest distress; while the accumulation of debt to the usurers became so heavy, that he was compelled to pass through the Insolvent Court. Thus ended the career of a man who had been courted in society, idolized in the army, and figured as a legislator for many years. His friends, of course, fell off, and he was to be seen a mendicant in the streets of London--shunned where he once was adored. Gray, his agent, became equally involved; but, marrying a widow with some money, he was enabled to make a better fight. Eventually, however, he became a prey to the money-lender, and his life ended under circumstances distressing to those who had known him in early days.

"MONK" LEWIS

One of the most agreeable men of the day was "Monk" Lewis. As the author of the Monk and the Tales of Wonder, he not only found his way into the best circles, but had gained a high reputation in the literary world. His poetic talent was undoubted, and he was intimately connected with Walter Scott in his ballad researches. His Alonzo the Brave and the Fair Imogene was recited at the theatres, and wherever he went he found a welcome reception. His West Indian fortune and connections, and his seat in Parliament, gave him access to all the aristocratic circles; from which, however, he was banished upon the appearance of the fourth and last dialogue of the Pursuits of Literature. Had a thunderbolt fallen upon him, he could not have been more astonished than he was by the onslaught of Mr. Matthias, which led to his ostracism from fashionable society.

It is not for me to appreciate the value of this satirical poem, which created such an extraordinary sensation, not only in the fashionable, but in the political world; I, however, remember that whilst at Canning's, at the Bishop of London's, and at Gifford's, it was pronounced the most classical and spirited production that had ever issued from the press, it was held up at Lord Holland's, at the Marquis of Lansdowne's, and at Brookes's, as one of the most spiteful and ill-natured satires that had ever disgraced the literary world; and one which no talent or classic lore could ever redeem. Certain it is, that Matthias fell foul of poor "Monk" Lewis for his romance: obscenity and blasphemy were the charges laid at his door; he was acknowledged to be a man of genius and fancy, but this added only to his crime, to which was superadded that of being a very young man. The charges brought against him cooled his friends and heated his enemies; the young ladies were forbidden to speak to him, matrons even feared him, and from being one of the idols of the world, he became one of the objects of its disdain. Even his father was led to believe that his son had abandoned the paths of virtue, and was on the high road to ruin.

"Monk" Lewis, unable to stand against the outcry thus raised against him, determined to try the effects of absence, and took his departure for the island in which his property was; but unfortunately for those who dissented from the ferocious judgment that was passed upon him, and for those who had discrimination enough to know that after all there was nothing very objectionable in his romance, and felt assured that posterity would do him justice, this amiable and kind-hearted man died on his passage out; leaving a blank in one variety of literature which has never been filled up.

The denunciation was not followed by any other severe criticism; but editors have, in compliance with the insinuations of Matthias, omitted the passages which he pointed out as objectionable, so that the original text is seldom met with.

"Monk" Lewis had a black servant, affectionately attached to his master; but so ridiculously did this servant repeat his master's expressions, that he became the laughing-stock of all his master's friends: Brummell used often to raise a hearty laugh at Carlton House by repeating witticisms which he pretended to have heard from Lewis's servant. Some of these were very stale; yet they were considered so good as to be repeated at the clubs, greatly adding to the reputation of the Beau as a teller of good things. "On one occasion," said Brummell, "I called to inquire after a young lady who had sprained her ancle; Lewis, on being asked how she was, had said in the black's presence, 'The doctor has seen her, put her legs straight, and the poor chicken is doing well.' The servant, therefore, told me, with a mysterious and knowing look, 'Oh, sir, the doctor has been here; she has laid eggs, and she and the chickens are doing well.'"

Such extravagances in those days were received as the essence of wit, and to such stories did the public give a willing ear, repeating them with unwearying zest. Even Sheridan's wit partook of this character, making him the delight of the Prince, who ruled over the fashionable world, and whose approbation was sufficient to give currency to anything, however ludicrous and absurd.

SIR THOMAS TURTON

There is a pleasure in recalling to memory even the school-boy pranks of men who make a figure in the world. The career of Turton promised to be a brilliant one; and had he not offended against the moral feeling of the country, and lost his position, he would have mounted to the highest step in the ladder of fortune. At Eton he showed himself a dashing and a daring boy, and was looked upon by Dr. Goodall, the then head master, as one of his best classical scholars; by his school-fellows he was even more highly regarded, being the acknowledged "cock of the school." Amongst the qualities that endeared him to them was a fearlessness which led him into dangers and difficulties, from which his pluck only could extricate him. He was a determined poacher: not one of the skulking class, but of a daring that led him to exert his abilities in Windsor Park itself; where he contrived to bag game, in spite of the watchfulness of the keepers and the surveillance of the well-paid watchers of the night. On one occasion; however, by some unlucky chance, tidings of his successes reached the ears of the royal gamekeeper, who formed a plan by which to entrap him; and so nearly were they pouncing upon Turton that he was obliged to take to his heels and fly, carrying with him a hare which he had caught. The keepers followed close upon his heels until they came to the Thames, into which Turton plunged, and, still holding his prize by his teeth, swam to the other side; to the astonishment and dismay of his pursuers, who had no inclination for a cold bath: their mortification was great at seeing Turton safely landed on the other side. He reached the college in safety; and the hare served for the enjoyment of merry friends.

Turton's history in after life I will not pursue; but must express my regret that he threw away golden opportunities of showing his love for classic lore, and his ability to meet the difficulties of life, in the same bold way in which he swam the Thames and baffled the Windsor gamekeepers.

GEORGE SMYTHE, THE LATE LORD STRANGFORD

This is another friend to whom I am pleased to pay the tribute of a reminiscence, and who, if he was not as well known as most of those I have spoken of, was yet highly prized by many of the most distinguished persons, and formed one of a circle that had great influence in England. Being the son of the well-known Lord Strangford, the translator of Camoens, he had a first place in aristocratic society, and had he not given himself up to indulgences and amusements, might have reached the rank of statesman. The late Lord Strangford was distinguished by those external qualifications which are everywhere acceptable; his manners were polished and easy, his conversation elegant and witty, and these, added to great personal attractions, gave him a charm which was generally felt. Disraeli, Sir Edward Bulwer Lytton, and the leading men of the day, were his associates. When Lord Aberdeen became Minister for Foreign Affairs he selected George Smythe as under secretary; in which capacity he acquitted himself with great ability. He could not, however, act under Lord Palmerston, and rather than do so gave up his position. He did not long survive, but died very young; just as he was beginning to learn the value of his rare abilities, and had ascertained how best they might have been of use to his country.

THE HONOURABLE GEORGE TALBOT

I have a very vivid recollection of George Talbot, a brother of the late Earl of Shrewsbury, and who was a fashionable man about town, of whom there are many anecdotes in circulation. The only one that took my fancy was related to me in Paris, where he was as usual in the midst of the gayest of the gay, recklessly spending his money, and oftentimes resorting for resources to the gambling-table, where at last he was thoroughly pigeoned.

Talbot had tried in vain all the usual means of recruiting his empty purse. Being a Roman Catholic, like most of the members of one of the oldest families in Great Britain, he was a regular attendant upon the ceremonies of his Church, and acquainted with all the clergy in Paris; so he took the resolution of going to his confessor, unburdening his conscience, and at the same time seeking counsel from the holy father, as to the best way of raising the wind. After entering minutely into his condition, and asking the priest how he could find funds to pay his debts and take him home, the confessor seemed touched by his tale of woe, and after much apparent consideration recommended him to trust in Providence. Talbot seemed struck with such sensible advice, and promised to call again in a few days. This second visit was made in due course; he again mourned over his condition, and requested the priest's advice and assistance. His story was listened to as before, with much commiseration, but he was again recommended to trust in Providence. Talbot came away quite crest-fallen, and evidently with little hope of any immediate relief. After the lapse of a few days, however, he appeared again before his confessor, apparently much elated, and invited the worthy abbe to dine with him at the Rocher du Cancale. This invitation was gladly accepted, the holy father not doubting but that he should have all the delicacies in the land, to which, in common with the rest of the clergy, he had no objection; nor was he disappointed. The dinner was recherche; the best the establishment could furnish was placed before them, and most heartily and lovingly did the worthy abbe devote himself to what was offered. At the end of the repast the carte a payer was duly furnished; but what was the astonishment of the reverend guest when Talbot declared that his purse was completely au sec, and that it had been a long time empty; but that upon this occasion, as upon all others, he trusted, as the abbe had advised him, in Providence. The Abbe Pecheron, recovering from his surprise, and being of a kind and generous disposition, laughed heartily at Talbot's impudence, and feeling that he had deserved this rebuke pulled out his purse, paid for the dinner, and did what he should have done at first--wrote to the members of Talbot's family, and obtained for him such assistance as enabled him to quit Paris and return home, where he afterwards led a more sober life.

A DINNER AT SIR JAMES BLAND BURGES'S, IN LOWER BROOK STREET; AUTUMN, 1815

I was once invited to dinner by Sir James Burges, father of my friend, Captain Burges, of the Guards: it was towards the end of the season 1815. I there met, to my great delight, Lord Byron and Sir Walter Scott; and amongst the rest of the company were Lord Caledon, and Croker, the Secretary to the Admiralty. Sir James had been private secretary to Pitt at the time of the French Revolution, and had a fund of curious anecdotes about everything and everybody of note at the end of the last century. I remember his telling us the now generally received story of Pitt dictating a King's speech off-hand--then a more difficult task than at the present day--without the slightest hesitation; this speech being adopted by his colleagues nearly word for word as it was written down.

Walter Scott was quite delightful, appearing full of fire and animation, and told some interesting anecdotes connected with his early life in Scotland. I remember his proving himself, what would have been called in the olden times he delighted to portray, "a stout trencher-man." Nor were his attentions confined by any means to the eatables; on the contrary, he showed himself worthy to have made a third in the famous carousal in Ivanhoe, between the Black Knight and the Holy Clerk of Copmanhurst.

Byron, whom I had before seen at the shooting galleries and elsewhere, was then a very handsome man, with remarkably fine eyes and hair; but was, as usual, all show-off and affectation. I recollect his saying that he disliked seeing women eat, or to have their company at dinner, from a wish to believe, if possible, in their more ethereal nature; but he was rallied into avowing that his chief dislike to their presence at the festive board arose from the fact of their being helped first, and consequently getting all the wings of the chickens, whilst men had to be content with the legs or other parts. Byron, on this occasion, was in great good humour, and full of boyish and even boisterous mirth.

Croker was also agreeable, notwithstanding his bitter and sarcastic remarks upon everything and everybody. The sneering, ill-natured expression of his face, struck me as an impressive contrast to the frank and benevolent countenance of Walter Scott.

I never assisted at a more agreeable dinner. According to the custom of the day, we sat late; the poets, statesmen, and soldiers, all drank an immense quantity of wine, and I for one felt the effects of it next day. Walter Scott gave one or two recitations, in a very animated manner, from the ballads that he had been collecting, which delighted his auditory; and both Lord Byron and Croker added to the hilarity of the evening by quotations from, and criticisms on the more prominent writers of the period.

LORD BYRON

I knew very little of Lord Byron personally, but lived much with two of his intimate friends, Scrope Davis and Wedderburn Webster; from whom I frequently heard many anecdotes of him. I regret that I remember so few; and wish that I had written down those told me by poor Scrope Davis, one of the most agreeable men I ever met.

When Byron was at Cambridge, he was introduced to Scrope Davis by their mutual friend, Matthews, who was afterwards drowned in the river Cam. After Matthews's death, Davis became Byron's particular friend, and was admitted to his rooms at all hours. Upon one occasion he found the poet in bed with his hair en papillote, upon which Scrope cried, "Ha, ha! Byron, I have at last caught you acting the part of the Sleeping Beauty."

Byron, in a rage, exclaimed, "No, Scrope; the part of a d----d fool, you should have said."

"Well, then, anything you please; but you have succeeded admirably in deceiving your friends, for it was my conviction that your hair curled naturally."

"Yes, naturally, every night," returned the poet; "but do not, my dear Scrope, let the cat out of the bag, for I am as vain of my curls as a girl of sixteen."

When in London, Byron used to go to Manton's shooting-gallery, in Davis street, to try his hand, as he said, at a wafer. Wedderburn Webster was present when the poet, intensely delighted with his own skill, boasted to Joe Manton that he considered himself the best shot in London. "No, my lord," replied Manton, "not the best; but your shooting, to-day, was respectable;" upon which Byron waxed wroth, and left the shop in a violent passion.

Lords Byron, Yarmouth, Pollington, Mountjoy, Walliscourt, Blandford, Captain Burges, Jack Bouverie, and myself, were in 1814, and for several years afterwards, amongst the chief and most constant frequenters of this well-known shooting-gallery, and frequently shot at the wafer for considerable sums of money. Manton was allowed to enter the betting list, and he generally backed me. On one occasion, I hit the wafer nineteen times out of twenty.

Byron lived a great deal at Brighton, his house being opposite the Pavilion. He was fond of boating, and was generally accompanied by a lad, who was said to be a girl in boy's clothes. This report was confirmed to me by Webster, who was then living at Brighton. The vivid description of the page in Lara, no doubt, gave some plausibility to this often-told tale. I myself witnessed the dexterous manner in which Byron used to get into his boat; for, while standing on the beach, I once saw him vault into it with the agility of a harlequin, in spite of his lame foot.

On one occasion, whilst his lordship was dining with a few of his friends in Charles Street, Pall Mall, a letter was delivered to Scrope Davis, which required an immediate answer. Scrope, after reading its contents, handed it to Lord Byron. It was thus worded:--

"MY DEAR SCROPE,--Lend me 500L. for a few days; the funds are shut for the dividends, or I would not have made this request.
"G. BRUMMELL."
The reply was:--
"My DEAR BRUMMELL,--All my money is locked up in the funds.
"SCROPE DAVIS."

This was just before Brummell's escape to the Continent.

I have frequently asked Scrope Davis his private opinion of Lord Byron, and invariably received the same answer--that he considered Lord Byron very agreeable and clever, but vain, overbearing, conceited, suspicious, and jealous. Byron hated Palmerston, but liked Peel, and thought that the whole world ought to be constantly employed in admiring his poetry and himself: he never could write a poem or a drama without making himself its hero, and he was always the subject of his own conversation.

During one of Henry Hobhouse's visits to Byron, at his villa near Genoa, and whilst they were walking in the garden, his lordship suddenly turned upon his guest, and, apropos of nothing, exclaimed, "Now, I know, Hobhouse, you are looking at my foot." Upon which Hobhouse kindly replied, "My dear Byron, nobody thinks of or looks at anything but your head."

SHELLEY

Shelley, the poet, cut off at so early an age; just when his great poetical talents had been matured by study and reflection, and when he probably would have produced some great work, was my friend and associate at Eton. He was a boy of studious and meditative habits, averse to all games and sports, and a great reader of novels and romances. He was a thin, slight lad, with remarkably lustrous eyes, fine hair, and a very peculiar shrill voice and laugh. His most intimate friend at Eton was a boy named Price, who was considered one of the best classical scholars amongst us. At his tutor, Bethell's, where he lodged, he attempted many mechanical and scientific experiments. By the aid of a common tinker, he contrived to make something like a steam-engine, which, unfortunately, one day suddenly exploded; to the great consternation of the neighbourhood and to the imminent danger of a severe flogging from Dr. Reate.

Soon after leaving school, and about the year 1810, he came, in a state of great distress and difficulty, to Swansea, when we had an opportunity of rendering him a service; but we never could ascertain what had brought him to Wales, though we had reason to suppose it was some mysterious affaire du coeur.

The last time I saw Shelley was at Genoa, in 1822, sitting on the sea-shore, and, when I came upon him, making a true poet's meal of bread and fruit; He at once recognized me, jumped up, and appearing greatly delighted, exclaimed, "Here you see me at my old Eton habits; but instead of the green fields for a couch, I have here the shores of the Mediterranean. It is very grand, and very romantic. I only wish I had some of the excellent brown bread and butter we used to get at Spiers's: but I was never very fastidious in my diet." Then he continued, in a wild and eccentric manner: "Gronow, do you remember the beautiful Martha, the Hebe of Spiers's? She was the loveliest girl I ever saw, and I loved her to distraction."

Shelley was looking careworn and ill; and, as usual, was very carelessly dressed. He had on a large and wide straw hat, his long brown hair, already streaked with grey, flowing in large masses from under it, and presented a wild and strange appearance.

During the time I sat by his side he asked many questions about myself and many of our schoolfellows; but on my questioning him in turn about himself, his way of life, and his future plans, he avoided entering into any explanation: indeed, he gave such short and evasive answers, that, thinking my inquisitiveness displeased him, I rose to take my leave. I observed that I had not been lucky enough to see Lord Byron in any of my rambles, to which he replied, "Byron is living at his villa, surrounded by his court of sycophants; but I shall shortly see him at Leghorn." We then shook hands. I never saw him again; for he was drowned shortly afterwards, with his friend, Captain Williams, and his body was washed ashore near Via Reggio. Every one is familiar with the romantic scene which took place on the sea-shore when the remains of my poor friend and Captain Williams were burnt, in the presence of Byron and Trelawney, in the Roman fashion. His ashes were gathered into an urn, and buried in the Protestant cemetery at Rome. He was but twenty-nine years of age at his death.

ROBERT SOUTHEY, THE POET

In the year 1803, my father received a letter of introduction from Mr. Rees, of the well-known firm of Longman, Paternoster Row, presenting Robert Southey, the poet, to him. He came into Wales with the hope of finding a cottage to reside in. Accordingly, a cavalcade was formed, consisting of Mr. W. Gwynne, the two brothers Southey, my father, and myself, and we rode up the Valley of Neath to look at a cottage about eight miles from the town. The poet, delighted with the scenery and situation, decided upon taking it; but the owner, unfortunately for the honour of

Welshmen, actually declined to let it to Robert Southey, fearing that a poet could not find security for the small annual rent of twenty-five pounds. This circumstance led the man of letters, who eventually became one of the most distinguished men of his day, to seek a home elsewhere, and the Lakes were at length chosen as his residence. Probably the picturesque beauties of Cumberland compensated the Laureate for the indignity put upon him by the Welshman.

An act of Vandalism perpetrated in the same Vale of Neath, and reflecting no honour on my countrymen, deserves here to be noted with reprobation. A natural cascade, called Dyllais, which was so beautiful as to excite the admiration of travellers, was destroyed by an agent to Lord Jersey, the proprietor of the estate, in order to build a few cottages and the lock of a canal. The rock down which this beautiful cascade had flowed from the time of the Flood, and which had created a scene of beauty universally admired, was blown up with gunpowder by this man, who could probably appreciate no more beautiful sight than that which presents itself from a window in Gray's or Lincoln's Inn, of which he was a member.

CAPTAIN HESSE, FORMERLY OF THE 18TH HUSSARS

One of my most intimate friends was the late Captain Hesse, generally believed to be a son of the Duke of York, by a German lady of rank. Though it is not my intention to disclose certain family secrets of which I am in possession, I may, nevertheless, record some circumstances connected with the life of my friend, which were familiar to a large circle with whom I mixed. Hesse, in early youth, lived with the Duke and Duchess of York; he was treated in such a manner by them as to indicate an interest in him by their Royal Highnesses which could scarcely be attributed to ordinary regard, and was gazetted a cornet in the 18th Hussars at seventeen years of age. Shortly afterwards, he went to Spain, and was present in all the battles in which his regiment was engaged; receiving a severe wound in the wrist at the battle of Vittoria. When this became known in England, a royal lady wrote to Lord Wellington, requesting that he might be carefully attended to; and, at the same time, a watch, with her portrait, was forwarded, which was delivered to the wounded Hussar by Lord Wellington himself. When he had sufficiently recovered, Hesse returned to England, and passed much of his time at Oatlands, the residence of the Duchess of York; he was also honoured with the confidence of the Princess Charlotte and her mother, Queen Caroline.

Many delicate and important transactions were conducted through the medium of Captain Hesse; in fact, it was perfectly well known that he played a striking part in many scenes of domestic life which I do not wish to reveal. I may, however, observe that the Prince Regent sent the late Admiral Lord Keith to Hesse's lodgings, who demanded, in his Royal Highness's name, the restitution of the watch and letters which had been sent him when in Spain. After a considerable amount of hesitation, the Admiral obtained what he wanted the following day; whereupon Lord Keith assured him that the Prince Regent would never forget so great a mark of confidence, and that the heir to the throne would ever afterwards be his friend. I regret to say, from personal knowledge, that, upon this occasion the Prince behaved most ungratefully and unfeelingly; for, after having obtained all he wanted, he positively refused to receive Hesse at Carlton House.

Hesse's life was full of singular incidents. He was a great friend of the Queen of Naples, grandmother of the ex-Sovereign of the Two Sicilies; in fact, so notorious was that liaison, that Hesse was eventually expelled from Naples under an escort of gendarmes. He was engaged in several affairs of honour, in which he always displayed the utmost courage; and his romantic career terminated by his being killed in a duel by Count L--, natural son of the first Napoleon. He died as he had lived, beloved by his friends, and leaving behind him little but his name and the kind thoughts of those who survived him.

VISITING IN THE COUNTRY

When I returned to London from Paris, in 1815, upon promotion, I was accompanied by Colonel Brooke, who was good enough to invite me to pass some time at his brother's, Sir R. Brookes, in Cheshire, upon the occasion of the christening of his eldest son. The fete was truly magnificent, and worthy of our excellent host; and all the great people of the neighbouring counties were present.

Soon afterwards I went to the Hale, a country house near Liverpool, belonging to Mr. Blackburn, one of the oldest members of the House of Commons, where many persons, who had been at Sir Richard Brookes's, met again. Mr. Blackburn was extremely absent and otherwise odd: upon one occasion I gave him a letter to frank, which he deliberately opened and read in my presence; and on my asking him if it amused him, he replied that he did not understand what it meant. Upon another occasion the Duke of Gloucester, accompanied by Mr. Blackburn, went out to shoot pheasants in the preserves near the Hale; when all of a sudden, Mr. B. observing that the Duke's gun was cocked, asked his Royal Highness whether he always carried his gun cocked. "Yes, Blackburn, always," was the reply.

"Well then, good morning, your Royal Highness; I will no longer accompany you."

At dinner Mr. Blackburn was very eccentric: he would never surrender his place at table even to royalty; so the Duke was obliged to sit near him. Whenever the royal servant filled the Duke's glass with wine and water, Mr. B. invariably drank it off; until at length, the Duke asked his servant for more wine and water, and anticipating a repetition of the farce that had so often been played, drank it off, and said, "Well, Blackburn, I have done you at last." After dinner the Duke and the men went to join the ladies in the drawing-room, where the servant in royal livery was waiting, holding a tray upon which was a cup of tea for the Duke. Mr. Blackburn, observing the servant in waiting, and that nobody took the cup of tea, determined on drinking it; but the domestic retired a little, to endeavour to prevent it. Mr. Blackburn, however, followed and persisted; Upon which the servant said, "Sir, it is for his Royal Highness."

"D---- his Royal Highness, I will have this tea."

The Duke exclaimed, "That's right, Blackburn," and ordered the servant to hand it to him.

COLONEL KELLY AND HIS BLACKING

Among the odd characters I have met with, I do not recollect anyone more eccentric than the late Lieutenant-colonel Kelly, of the First Foot Guards, who was the vainest man I ever encountered. He was a thin, emaciated-looking dandy, but had all the bearing of the gentleman. He was haughty in the extreme, and very fond of dress; his boots were so well varnished that the polish now in use could not surpass Kelly's blacking in brilliancy; his pantaloons were made of the finest leather, and his coats were inimitable: in short, his dress was considered perfect.

His sister held the place of housekeeper to the Custom-house, and when it was burnt down, Kelly was burnt with it, in endeavoring to save his favorite boots. When the news of his horrible death became known, all the dandies were anxious to secure the services of his valet, who possessed the mystery of the inimitable blacking. Brummell lost no time in discovering his place of residence, and asked what wages he required; the servant answered, his late master gave him 150L. a-year, but it was not enough for his talents, and he should require 200L.; upon which Brummell said, "well, if you will make it guineas, I shall be happy to attend upon you." The late Lord Plymouth eventually secured this phoenix of valets at 200L. a-year, and bore away the sovereignty of boots.

LORD ALLEN AND COUNT D'ORSAY

Lord Allen being rather the worse for drinking too much wine at dinner, teased Count D'Orsay, and said some very disagreeable things, which irritated him; when suddenly John Bush entered the club and shook hands with the Count, who exclaimed, "Voila, la difference entre une bonne bouche et une mauvaise haleine."

The following bon mot was also attributed to the Count: General Ornano, observing a certain nobleman--who, by some misfortune in his youth, lost the use of his legs--in a Bath chair, which he wheeled about, and inquiring the name of the English peer, D'Orsay answered, "Pere la Chaise."

The Count had many disciples among our men of fashion, but none of them succeeded in copying the original. His death produced, both in London and in Paris, a deep and universal regret. The Count's life has been so well delineated in the public prints, that nothing I could say would add to the praise that has been bestowed upon him. Perfectly natural in manners and language, highly accomplished, and never betraying the slightest affectation or pretension, he had formed friendships with some of the noblest and most accomplished men in England. He was also a great favourite in Paris, where he had begun to exercise his talent as an artist, when death prematurely removed him from society.

Mr. PHELPS

Mr. Phelps, a chorus singer, and an excellent musician, with good looks and address, contrived to ingratiate himself with the Marchioness of Antrim, and was fortunate enough to marry her ladyship, by whose means he was created a baronet, and allied to some of our most aristocratic families.

THE LATE LORD BLOOMFIELD

The late Lord Bloomfield likewise owed his elevation to the Peerage to his musical talents. When the Prince of Wales was living at the Pavilion at Brighton, he wanted some one who could accompany him on the violoncello, and having ascertained that Captain Bloomfield, of the Royal Artillery, who was then at Brighton with his troop, was an accomplished violoncello player, the captain was accordingly summoned to appear before the Prince, at the Pavilion. From that night commenced an intimacy which for many years existed between the Prince and Captain Bloomfield; who for a considerable length of time was well known in fashionable circles under the title of Sir Benjamin Bloomfield. A court intrigue, headed by a fascinating marchioness, caused him to be sent into splendid exile: this lady attributing to Sir Benjamin Bloomfield her being compelled to send back some jewels which had been presented to her by the Prince Regent; but which, it was discovered, belonged to the Crown, and could not be alienated. Sir Benjamin was created a Peer, and sent to Stockholm as ambassador, where his affable manners and his unostentatious hospitality rendered him exceedingly popular; and he became as great a favorite with Bernadotte as he had been with the Prince Regent. The name of Bloomfield is at this day respected in Sweden.

THE RIGHT HON. GEORGE CANNING

When Mr. Canning retired from Portugal, he was received at Paris with a distinction and a deference perhaps never before bestowed on a foreign diplomatist; he dined with Charles X. almost tete-a-tete, and was scrambled for by the leading aristocracy of France. It happened that he also dined, on one occasion, with the Bailly Ferret, who was the oldest foreign ambassador in Paris; and it was generally understood that Canning, who had the reputation of being a gourmand, and was not in robust health at the time, never thoroughly recovered from these Parisian hospitalities. A short time after, this great orator, and the most brilliant statesman of the day, breathed his last at Chiswick, in the same room in which Charles James Fox died.

MRS. BOEHM, OF ST. JAMES'S SQUARE

This lady used to give fashionable balls and masquerades, to which I look back with much pleasure. The Prince Regent frequently honoured her fetes with his presence. Mrs. Boehm, on one occasion, sent invitations to one of her particular friends, begging him to fill them up, and tickets were given by him to Dick Butler (afterwards Lord Glengal) and to Mr. Raikes. Whilst they were deliberating in what character they should go, Dick Butler--for by that name he was only then known--proposed that Raikes should take the part of Apollo; which the latter agreed to, provided Dick would be his lyre. The noble lord's reputation for stretching the long bow rendered this repartee so applicable, that it was universally repeated at the clubs.

DR. GOODALL, OF ETON

This gentleman was proverbially fond of punning. About the same time that he was made Provost of Eton, he received, also, a Stall at Windsor. A young lady of his acquaintance, while congratulating him on his elevation, and requesting him to give the young ladies of Eton and Windsor a ball during the vacation, happened to touch his wig with her fan, and caused the powder to fly about. Upon which the doctor exclaimed, "My dear, you see you can get the powder out of the canon, but not the ball."

LORD MELBOURNE, THE DUKE OF LEINSTER, AND LORD NORMANBY

When Lord Melbourne offered the garter to the Duke of Leinster, his grace is reported to have answered that he did not want it; adding, "It will, no doubt, be eagerly accepted by one of your lordship's supporters in the Upper House." On another occasion, when Lord Normanby was soliciting Lord Melbourne to be made a marquis, the noble Premier observed, in his jocular way, "Why, Normanby, you are not such a d----d fool as to want that!" The favour, however, was eventually granted.

THE DUKE OF GLOUCESTER

His Royal Highness, who was in the habit of saying very ludicrous things, asked one of his friends in the House of Lords, on the occasion when William IV. assented to Lord Grey's Proposition to pass the Reform Bill coute qui coute, "Who is Silly Billy now?" This was in allusion to the general opinion that was prevalent of the Royal Duke's weakness, and which had obtained for him the sobriquet of "Silly Billy."

The Duke frequently visited Cheltenham during the season. Upon one occasion, he called upon Colonel Higgins, brother to the equerry of his Royal Highness the Prince Regent, and, on inquiring of the servant if his master was at home, received for answer, "My master is dying."

"Dying!" repeated the Duke; "have you sent for a doctor?"

"No, sir."

His Royal Highness immediately ran back into the street, and, having the good fortune to find a medical man, he requested him to come at once to Colonel Higgins, as he was on the point of death. The Duke and the doctor soon reached the colonel's house, and, after again asking the servant how his master was, that functionary replied, "I told you, sir, that he is dying." They mounted the staircase, and were rather amused to find the reported invalid busily occupied in dyeing his hair.

LADY CORK

In 1819, this venerable lady lived in Old Burlington Street, where she gave many parties, to persons of all nations, and contrived to bring together foreigners from the wilds of America, the Cape of Good Hope, and even savages from the isles of the Pacific; in fact, she was the notorious lion-hunter of her age. It was supposed that she had a peculiar ignorance of the laws of meum and tuum, and that her monomania was such that she would try to get possession of whatever she could place her hands upon; so that it was dangerous to leave in the ante-room anything of value. On application being made, however, the articles were usually returned the following day, the fear of the law acting strongly upon her ladyship's bewildered brain.

THE DUCHESS OF GORDON

This leader of fashion, who was wont to be the admiration of all circles, was looked upon as the most ambitious of women, and her vanity was fully gratified by the marriage of her daughters to the first people in the realm--the Dukes of Richmond, Manchester, and Bedford, and the Marquis of Cornwallis.

THE LATE MRS. BRADSHAW (MARIA TREE)

The two Miss Trees, Maria and Ellen (the latter now Mrs. Kean), were the great favourites of the Bath Stage for many seasons before they became leading stars in London. Miss Ellen Tree made her first appearance in a grand entertainment, called the Cataract of the Ganges, in a magnificent car drawn by six horses. Her beauty made a deep impression on the audience, which was naturally increased by her subsequent exhibition of great talents.

Miss Maria Tree was much admired as a vocalist, and her Viola, in Twelfth Night, was one of the most popular performances of the day. Mr. Bradshaw became desperately enamoured of her during her engagement in London, and having learnt that she was about to go by the mail coach to Birmingham, where she was to perform her principal characters, thought it a favourable opportunity of enjoying her society; so he sent his servant to secure him a place by the mail, under the name of Tomkins. At the appointed time for departure, Mr. Bradshaw was at the office, and jumping into the coach was soon whirled away; but great was his disappointment at finding that the fair object of his admiration was not a fellow-passenger: he was not consoled by discovering that there were two mails, the one the Birmingham, mail, the other the Birmingham and Manchester, and that whilst he was journeying by the latter, Miss Tree was travelling in the other.

On arriving at Birmingham, early in the morning, he left the coach and stepped into the hotel, determined to remain there, and go to the theatre on the following evening. He went to bed, and slept late the following day; and on waking he remembered that his trunk with all his money had gone on to Manchester, and that he was without the means of paying his way. Seeing the Bank of Birmingham opposite the hotel, he went over and explained his position to one of the partners, giving his own banker's address in London, and showing letters addressed to him as Mr. Bradshaw. Upon this he was told that with such credentials he might have a loan; and the banker said he would write the necessary letter and cheque, and send the money over to him at the hotel. Mr. Bradshaw, pleased with this kind attention, sat himself down comfortably to breakfast in the coffee-room. According to promise, the cashier made his appearance at the hotel, and asked the waiter for Mr. Bradshaw.

"No such gentleman here," was the reply.

"Oh, yes, he came by the London mail."

"No, sir; no one came but Mr. Tomkins, who was booked as inside passenger to Manchester."

The cashier was dissatisfied; but the waiter added, "Sir, you can look through the window of the coffee-room door, and see the gentleman yourself."

On doing so, he beheld the Mr. Tomkins, alias Mr. Bradshaw, and immediately returned to the Bank, telling what he himself had heard and seen. The banker went over to the hotel, had a consultation with the landlord, and it was determined that a watch should be placed upon the suspicious person who had two names and no luggage, and who was booked to Manchester but had stopped at Birmingham.

The landlord summoned boots--a little lame fellow, of most ludicrous appearance,--and pointing to the gentleman in the coffee-room, told him his duty for the day was to follow him wherever he went, and never to lose sight of him; but above all to take care that he did not get away. Boots nodded assent, and immediately mounted guard. Mr. Bradshaw having taken his breakfast and read the papers, looked at his watch, and sallied forth to see something of the goodly town of Birmingham. He was much surprised at observing a little odd-looking man surveying him most attentively, and watching his every movement; stopping whenever he stopped, and evidently taking a deep interest in all he did. At last, observing that he was the object of this incessant espionage, and finding that he had a shilling left in his pocket, he hailed one of the coaches that ran short distances in those days when omnibuses were not. This, however, did not suit little boots, who went up to him and insisted that he must not leave the town.

Mr. Bradshaw's indignation was naturally excessive, and he immediately returned to the hotel, where he found a constable ready to take him before the mayor as an impostor and swindler. He was compelled to appear before his worship, and had the mortification of being told that unless he could give some explanation, he must be content with a night's lodging in a house of detention. Mr. Bradshaw had no alternative but to send to the fair charmer of his heart to identify him; which she most readily did, as soon as rehearsal was over. Explanations were then entered into; but he was forced to give the reason of his being in Birmingham, which of course made a due impression on the lady's heart, and led to that happy result of their interviews--a marriage which resulted in the enjoyment of mutual happiness for many years.

LADIES' JEWELLERY AND LOVERS

Some of the most magnificent fortunes of England have, in the first instance, been undermined by an extravagant expenditure on jewellery, which has been given to ladies, married and unmarried, who have fascinated their wealthy admirers and made them their slaves. Hamlet, and Rundell and Bridge, were in my day patronized by the great, and obtained large sums of money from their enamoured clients, to whom they often became bankers.

On the day after the coronation of George IV., Hamlet made his appearance at the house of Mr. Coutts, in Piccadilly, the corner of Stratton Street. It was during dinner; but, owing no doubt to a previous arrangement, he was at once admitted, when he placed before the rich banker a magnificent diamond cross, which had been worn the previous day by the Duke of York. It at once attracted the admiration of Mrs. Coutts, who loudly exclaimed, "How happy I should be with such a splendid specimen of jewellery." "What is it worth?" immediately exclaimed Mr. Coutts. "I could not allow it to pass out of my possession for less than 15,000L.," said the wary tradesman. "Bring me a pen and ink," was the only answer made by the doting husband; and he at once drew a cheque for that amount upon the bank in the Strand; and with much delight the worthy old gentleman placed the jewel upon the fair bosom of the lady:

"Upon her breast a sparkling cross she wore,
Which Jews might kiss, and infidels adore."

The Earl of C--, whose reputation in the sporting world was of the highest order, and who had obtained some notoriety by his amours, fell into the hands of Hamlet, who was known to the aristocracy by his mock title of "Prince of Denmark." Hamlet placed before him, on one occasion, jewels to the amount of thirty thousand pounds, and volunteered, as his client was not of age, to give him credit for several months. The offer was accepted, and the brilliant present became the possession of a young lady, one of the Terpsichorean tribe (Mademoiselle Le G.), whose charms had captivated the youthful nobleman, and who had so irrevocably fascinated him by the expression of her love, awakened by the prospect of a rich remuneration, that she accepted him as the sole possessor of a heart which had been before at the disposal of any rich admirer whose purse was worthy her consideration.

This lady, who is now somewhat advanced in years, but has still the remains of beauty, is living in France upon her estate; the produce of the many charms which she once possessed, and which she turned to such advantage, as to make her society even up to this day courted by those who look upon wealth as the great source of distinction, and who are willing to disbelieve any stories that they may accidentally hear of her previous history.

THE LATE LORD HENRY SEYMOUR

I knew Lord Henry perhaps better than any other Englishman, having lived with him on terms of great intimacy. He was famous for his racing stud and good taste in his carriages and riding-horses. It was said, by persons who were little acquainted with him, that he was fond of masquerades, fighting, and was also the terror of pugilists, from his great strength and science in boxing; on the contrary, he was a gentle, retiring, and humane man, and never was known to have been present at a masquerade, or any place of the sort. But it unfortunately happened that a man named "Franconi," of the Circus--a low-born and vulgar fellow--resembled him in looks and stature, and having been mistaken for my noble friend gave himself out as Lord Seymour in those dens of infamy, where the noble lord was unknown.

Lord Henry was a man of fine taste, and fond of the arts, and, at his death, his paintings, library, and plate fetched a considerable sum at public auction. During his lifetime he patronized young artists: often advancing them money, and assisting them in every possible way.

Lord Henry Seymour was the founder of the French Jockey Club, and, in conjunction with the late Duke de Gramont (better known in England as the Count de Guiche), made racing in France what it now is: that is, they placed the turf upon a respectable footing. Lord Henry established a school of arms and gymnasium in his hotel on the Boulevard des Italiens, which became the most celebrated in Europe. He himself was an adept in the art of fencing, his skill was considered by the professors to be incomparable.

His kindness of heart and unostentatious generosity were his noblest qualities. One morning, whilst we were breakfasting in his library, a friend entered, and, with a sad countenance, informed Lord Henry that he had that morning been visiting an old friend of his, a man of good birth, who, with his wife and children, were absolutely starving, and that they were reduced to sleep upon straw. Lord Henry, touched by this painful information, asked where those poor people were to be found, and being told, he said not a word more, but ordered his carriage and went out. The next morning the same gentleman made his appearance, and said, "I call to tell you, Seymour, that I am just come from my poor friend, who, I am happy to say, has received relief, in the shape of furniture, bedding, linen, and food, from some kind person, who also left a considerable sum of money to purchase wearing apparel for the family."

Seymour never moved a muscle of his face, and we were wondering from whence the relief came, when a fine-looking fellow entered, bowing in the most respectful manner, and addressed his lordship in the following terms:--"My lord, I am obliged to confess that I have taken some trouble to discover the name of our benefactor, and, from all I have been able to learn, it cannot be any other than your lordship; I therefore deem it my duty, on behalf of my wife, children, and self, to return you my heartfelt thanks for this unexampled act of charity towards a perfect stranger." The poor fellow shed tears in thus addressing his lordship, who kindly gave him his hand, and promised to be his friend for the future; which promise he fulfilled, by procuring him a place under the Government, that enabled him to live happily and bring up his family with honour and comfort.

FRANCE AND THE FRENCH

I will not permit this little volume to make its appearance in English society, without a few words about a people with whom I have mingled for nearly forty years. When I first came to France, few of my countrypeople travelled, save those belonging to the rich and aristocratic classes; it was not, therefore, surprising that those whose interest it might have been, on both sides of the Channel, to create a bad feeling between England and France, found little difficulty in doing so. An Englishman was taught to hate the French as well as to observe the Ten Commandments; and a Frenchman, on the other hand, was educated with the idea that his only enemy on the face of the earth was an Englishman.

I regard this stimulated hostile feeling between two nations which must ever influence the welfare of the human race more than any others, as one of the greatest calamities that could curse humanity. We have only to read history from the days of Agincourt up to our later struggles with Napoleon I., to come to the conclusion that the two bravest and the most intelligent nations on the face of the earth have, from DYNASTIC ambition, and a want of the people knowing each other, been ever engaged in inflicting mutual disasters, which have impeded for centuries the progress, civilization, and prosperity of both; whilst the want of a proper understanding between the two countries has materially aided in retarding other nations in obtaining that political emancipation necessary to the happiness of mankind.

I have lived through a period characterized by sanguinary wars and huge national debts, and have remained in this world long enough to calculate their results. I am afraid we must often be content with that empty glory which lives only in the pages of history. A battle fought fifty years ago appears very often of no more utility than the splendid tomb of a Necropolis. Events and objects for which men by thousands were brought together in deadly combat assume, a few years afterwards, mighty small proportions; and those who have taken part in deadly struggles, at a later period marvel at the enthusiasm which then animated them. I am no believer in that era of happiness which some divines imagine to be so near at hand; nor do I imagine that the next two or three hundred years will witness the sword turned into the reaping-hook of peaceful industry; but what I do believe in, and what I hope for, is that nations will know each other better than they did of old. It will be more difficult for sovereigns and governments to bring about wars between neighboring nations now, than it was before the existence of that intercommunication which in our day has been created by the press, the railway, and the electric telegraph.

I have lived long enough to find hundreds of my countrymen participating in a real knowledge of the French, and believing with me that they are a brave, intelligent, and generous nation. Nearly half a century of experience amongst them has taught me that there is much to learn and much that is worthy of imitation in France. The social habits of the French, and their easy mode of communication, always gain the admiration, and often invite the attachment of foreigners. They are less prejudiced than we islanders, and are much more citizens of the world than ourselves. I have received an immense amount of courtesy in France; and if there be less of solid friendship--which, however, in England is based too often on a similarity of birth, position, and wealth--in France, you have, at least, a greater chance than in England of making a friend of a man who neither looks to your ancestors nor your amount of riches before he proffers you the most sincere intimacy, and, if necessary, disinterested aid, purely on the ground of your own merit and character.

Many of the better qualities of the French are not discoverable by the superficial traveller, any more than the sterling qualities of the Englishman are appreciated by the foreigner who makes a brief sojourn in Great Britain. Slowly, but, I believe, surely, the agreeable knowledge that I possess of the French is becoming more universal; and I cannot but imagine that such a correct appreciation will be fraught with the most valuable political as well as social results.

Intelligent Englishmen have lived long enough to appreciate the genius of Napoleon I., whose mode of governing France has been applied by Napoleon III. with a success which prejudice even has been compelled to acknowledge. But I remember a period when probably not a dozen Englishmen could have been found to speak of the first Emperor with the most ordinary common sense. I will, however, record one honourable exception to the rule. The late Lord Dudley and Ward, an eccentric, but able man, was at Vienna, in the midst of a large party, who were all more or less abusing or depreciating the fallen hero, whose very name had so long created fear and hatred amongst them. It was naturally supposed that the Englishman who was silently listening to this conversation must of course, as the natural enemy of France, approve of all that had been said. Prince Metternich turned at last to his guest, and said, "Et vous, my Lord, que pensez vous de Napoleon?" "Je pense," replied Lord Dudley, "qu'il a rendu la gloire passee douteuse, et la renommee future impossible."

As an old soldier and an admirer of the Duke of Wellington, I cannot altogether admit the entire justice of the observation; yet, spoken by an Englishman to the enemies of the exiled Emperor, it was a gallant homage paid to fallen greatness.

The great man who now wields the destinies of France possesses many of the remarkable qualities of the founder of his dynasty: his energetic will, his extensive and varied knowledge, his aptitude for government, his undaunted bravery, and that peculiar tact which leads him to say the right thing at the right time. But to these rare gifts he joins the most princely generosity, and a kind and gentle heart: he has never been known to forsake a friend, or leave unrewarded any proofs of devotion shown to him in his days of exile. He is adored by the vast majority of the French nation, and even his political opponents, if accidentally brought under the influence of his particularly winning and gracious manner, are, in spite of themselves, charmed and softened.

There can be no doubt that Napoleon III. enjoys a well-merited popularity, and that there is throughout all classes a deep and earnest confidence that the honour and glory of France are safe in his hands.

It is just this mighty power, founded on the love and trust of his people, which is the surest pledge that peace will be maintained between our country and France. Napoleon III. does not require to court popularity by pandering to the anti-English prejudices still retained by a small minority of his subjects; and, unlike the representatives of less popular dynasties, he can afford to show that he is not only the beloved and mighty ruler of the French nation, but also the firm ally and faithful friend of England.

www.bookjungle.com *email: sales@bookjungle.com fax: 630-214-0564 mail: Book Jungle PO Box 2226 Champaign, IL 61825*

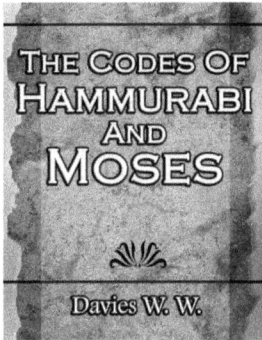

The Codes Of Hammurabi And Moses
W. W. Davies

QTY

The discovery of the Hammurabi Code is one of the greatest achievements of archaeology, and is of paramount interest, not only to the student of the Bible, but also to all those interested in ancient history...

Religion   **ISBN:** *1-59462-338-4*   **Pages:132**
MSRP $12.95

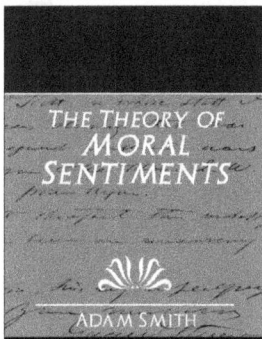

The Theory of Moral Sentiments
Adam Smith

QTY

This work from 1749. contains original theories of conscience amd moral judgment and it is the foundation for systemof morals.

Philosophy **ISBN:** *1-59462-777-0*   **Pages:536**
MSRP $19.95

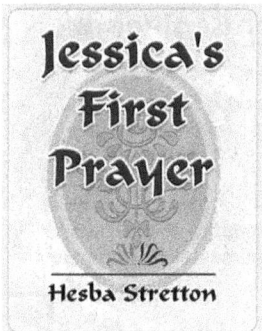

Jessica's First Prayer
Hesba Stretton

QTY

In a screened and secluded corner of one of the many railway-bridges which span the streets of London there could be seen a few years ago, from five o'clock every morning until half past eight, a tidily set-out coffee-stall, consisting of a trestle and board, upon which stood two large tin cans, with a small fire of charcoal burning under each so as to keep the coffee boiling during the early hours of the morning when the work-people were thronging into the city on their way to their daily toil...

Pages:84

Childrens   **ISBN:** *1-59462-373-2*   *MSRP $9.95*

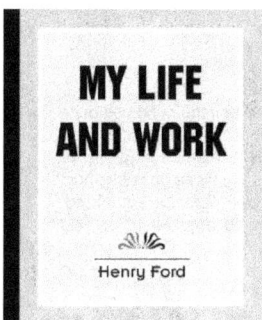

My Life and Work
Henry Ford

QTY

Henry Ford revolutionized the world with his implementation of mass production for the Model T automobile. Gain valuable business insight into his life and work with his own auto-biography... "We have only started on our development of our country we have not as yet, with all our talk of wonderful progress, done more than scratch the surface. The progress has been wonderful enough but..."

Pages:300

Biographies/   **ISBN:** *1-59462-198-5*   *MSRP $21.95*

www.bookjungle.com *email: sales@bookjungle.com fax: 630-214-0564 mail: Book Jungle PO Box 2226 Champaign, IL 61825*

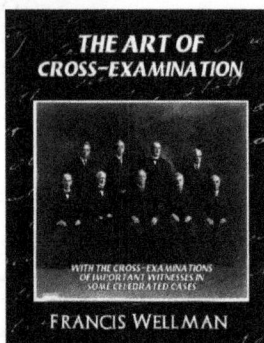

The Art of Cross-Examination
Francis Wellman

I presume it is the experience of every author, after his first book is published upon an important subject, to be almost overwhelmed with a wealth of ideas and illustrations which could readily have been included in his book, and which to his own mind, at least, seem to make a second edition inevitable. Such certainly was the case with me; and when the first edition had reached its sixth impression in five months, I rejoiced to learn that it seemed to my publishers that the book had met with a sufficiently favorable reception to justify a second and considerably enlarged edition. ..

Pages:412

Reference   **ISBN: *1-59462-647-2***   *MSRP $19.95*

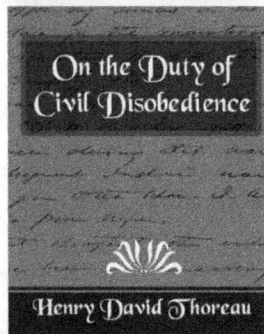

On the Duty of Civil Disobedience
Henry David Thoreau

Thoreau wrote his famous essay, On the Duty of Civil Disobedience, as a protest against an unjust but popular war and the immoral but popular institution of slave-owning. He did more than write—he declined to pay his taxes, and was hauled off to gaol in consequence. Who can say how much this refusal of his hastened the end of the war and of slavery ?

Law   **ISBN: *1-59462-747-9***   **Pages:48**

MSRP $7.45

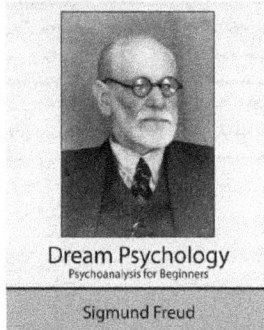

Dream Psychology Psychoanalysis for Beginners
Sigmund Freud

Sigmund Freud, born Sigismund Schlomo Freud (May 6, 1856 - September 23, 1939), was a Jewish-Austrian neurologist and psychiatrist who co-founded the psychoanalytic school of psychology. Freud is best known for his theories of the unconscious mind, especially involving the mechanism of repression; his redefinition of sexual desire as mobile and directed towards a wide variety of objects; and his therapeutic techniques, especially his understanding of transference in the therapeutic relationship and the presumed value of dreams as sources of insight into unconscious desires.

Pages:196

Psychology   **ISBN: *1-59462-905-6***   *MSRP $15.45*

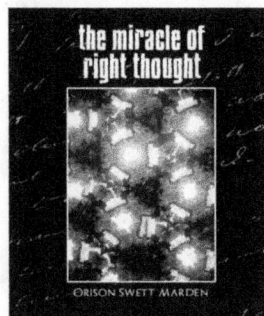

The Miracle of Right Thought
Orison Swett Marden

Believe with all of your heart that you will do what you were made to do. When the mind has once formed the habit of holding cheerful, happy, prosperous pictures, it will not be easy to form the opposite habit. It does not matter how improbable or how far away this realization may see, or how dark the prospects may be, if we visualize them as best we can, as vividly as possible, hold tenaciously to them and vigorously struggle to attain them, they will gradually become actualized, realized in the life. But a desire, a longing without endeavor, a yearning abandoned or held indifferently will vanish without realization.

Pages:360

Self Help   **ISBN: *1-59462-644-8***   *MSRP $25.45*

QTY

The Rosicrucian Cosmo-Conception Mystic Christianity *by Max Heindel* ISBN: *1-59462-188-8* **$38.95**
The Rosicrucian Cosmo-conception is not dogmatic, neither does it appeal to any other authority than the reason of the student. It is: not controversial, but is: sent forth in the, hope that it may help to clear... *New Age/Religion Pages 646*

Abandonment To Divine Providence *by Jean-Pierre de Caussade* ISBN: *1-59462-228-0* **$25.95**
"The Rev. Jean Pierre de Caussade was one of the most remarkable spiritual writers of the Society of Jesus in France in the 18th Century. His death took place at Toulouse in 1751. His works have gone through many editions and have been republished... *Inspirational/Religion Pages 400*

Mental Chemistry *by Charles Haanel* ISBN: *1-59462-192-6* **$23.95**
Mental Chemistry allows the change of material conditions by combining and appropriately utilizing the power of the mind. Much like applied chemistry creates something new and unique out of careful combinations of chemicals the mastery of mental chemistry... *New Age Pages 354*

The Letters of Robert Browning and Elizabeth Barret Barrett 1845-1846 vol II ISBN: *1-59462-193-4* **$35.95**
by Robert Browning and Elizabeth Barrett *Biographies Pages 596*

Gleanings In Genesis (volume I) *by Arthur W. Pink* ISBN: *1-59462-130-6* **$27.45**
Appropriately has Genesis been termed "the seed plot of the Bible" for in it we have, in germ form, almost all of the great doctrines which are afterwards fully developed in the books of Scripture which follow... *Religion/Inspirational Pages 420*

The Master Key *by L. W. de Laurence* ISBN: *1-59462-001-6* **$30.95**
In no branch of human knowledge has there been a more lively increase of the spirit of research during the past few years than in the study of Psychology, Concentration and Mental Discipline. The requests for authentic lessons in Thought Control, Mental Discipline and... *New Age/Business Pages 422*

The Lesser Key Of Solomon Goetia *by L. W. de Laurence* ISBN: *1-59462-092-X* **$9.95**
This translation of the first book of the "Lernegton" which is now for the first time made accessible to students of Talismanic Magic was done, after careful collation and edition, from numerous Ancient Manuscripts in Hebrew, Latin, and French... *New Age/Occult Pages 92*

Rubaiyat Of Omar Khayyam *by Edward Fitzgerald* ISBN:*1-59462-332-5* **$13.95**
Edward Fitzgerald, whom the world has already learned, in spite of his own efforts to remain within the shadow of anonymity, to look upon as one of the rarest poets of the century, was born at Bredfield, in Suffolk, on the 31st of March, 1809. He was the third son of John Purcell... *Music Pages 172*

Ancient Law *by Henry Maine* ISBN: *1-59462-128-4* **$29.95**
The chief object of the following pages is to indicate some of the earliest ideas of mankind, as they are reflected in Ancient Law, and to point out the relation of those ideas to modern thought. *Religion/History Pages 452*

Far-Away Stories *by William J. Locke* ISBN: *1-59462-129-2* **$19.45**
"Good wine needs no bush, but a collection of mixed vintages does. And this book is just such a collection. Some of the stories I do not want to remain buried for ever in the museum files of dead magazine-numbers an author's not unpardonable vanity..." *Fiction Pages 272*

Life of David Crockett *by David Crockett* ISBN: *1-59462-250-7* **$27.45**
"Colonel David Crockett was one of the most remarkable men of the times in which he lived. Born in humble life, but gifted with a strong will, an indomitable courage, and unremitting perseverance... *Biographies/New Age Pages 424*

Lip-Reading *by Edward Nitchie* ISBN: *1-59462-206-X* **$25.95**
Edward B. Nitchie, founder of the New York School for the Hard of Hearing, now the Nitchie School of Lip-Reading, Inc, wrote "LIP-READING Principles and Practice". The development and perfecting of this meritorious work on lip-reading was an undertaking... *How-to Pages 400*

A Handbook of Suggestive Therapeutics, Applied Hypnotism, Psychic Science ISBN: *1-59462-214-0* **$24.95**
by Henry Munro *Health/New Age/Health/Self-help Pages 376*

A Doll's House: and Two Other Plays *by Henrik Ibsen* ISBN: *1-59462-112-8* **$19.95**
Henrik Ibsen created this classic when in revolutionary 1848 Rome. Introducing some striking concepts in playwriting for the realist genre, this play has been studied the world over. *Fiction/Classics/Plays 308*

The Light of Asia *by sir Edwin Arnold* ISBN: *1-59462-204-3* **$13.95**
In this poetic masterpiece, Edwin Arnold describes the life and teachings of Buddha. The man who was to become known as Buddha to the world was born as Prince Gautama of India but he rejected the worldly riches and abandoned the reigns of power when... *Religion/History/Biographies Pages 170*

The Complete Works of Guy de Maupassant *by Guy de Maupassant* ISBN: *1-59462-157-8* **$16.95**
"For days and days, nights and nights, I had dreamed of that first kiss which was to consecrate our engagement, and I knew not on what spot I should put my lips..." *Fiction/Classics Pages 240*

The Art of Cross-Examination *by Francis L. Wellman* ISBN: *1-59462-309-0* **$26.95**
Written by a renowned trial lawyer, Wellman imparts his experience and uses case studies to explain how to use psychology to extract desired information through questioning. *How-to/Science/Reference Pages 408*

Answered or Unanswered? *by Louisa Vaughan* ISBN: *1-59462-248-5* **$10.95**
Miracles of Faith in China *Religion Pages 112*

The Edinburgh Lectures on Mental Science (1909) *by Thomas* ISBN: *1-59462-008-3* **$11.95**
This book contains the substance of a course of lectures recently given by the writer in the Queen Street Hail, Edinburgh. Its purpose is to indicate the Natural Principles governing the relation between Mental Action and Material Conditions... *New Age/Psychology Pages 148*

Ayesha *by H. Rider Haggard* ISBN: *1-59462-301-5* **$24.95**
Verily and indeed it is the unexpected that happens! Probably if there was one person upon the earth from whom the Editor of this, and of a certain previous history, did not expect to hear again... *Classics Pages 380*

Ayala's Angel *by Anthony Trollope* ISBN: *1-59462-352-X* **$29.95**
The two girls were both pretty, but Lucy who was twenty-one who supposed to be simple and comparatively unattractive, whereas Ayala was credited, as her Bombwhat romantic name might show, with poetic charm and a taste for romance. Ayala when her father died was nineteen... *Fiction Pages 484*

The American Commonwealth *by James Bryce* ISBN: *1-59462-286-8* **$34.45**
An interpretation of American democratic political theory. It examines political mechanics and society from the perspective of Scotsman James Bryce *Politics Pages 572*

Stories of the Pilgrims *by Margaret P. Pumphrey* ISBN: *1-59462-116-0* **$17.95**
This book explores pilgrims religious oppression in England as well as their escape to Holland and eventual crossing to America on the Mayflower, and their early days in New England... *History Pages 268*

www.bookjungle.com *email: sales@bookjungle.com fax: 630-214-0564 mail: Book Jungle PO Box 2226 Champaign, IL 61825*

QTY

The Fasting Cure *by Sinclair Upton*   ISBN: *1-59462-222-1*   **$13.95**
In the Cosmopolitan Magazine for May, 1910, and in the Contemporary Review (London) for April, 1910, I published an article dealing with my experiences in fasting. I have written a great many magazine articles, but never one which attracted so much attention...   New Age/Self Help/Health Pages 164

Hebrew Astrology *by Sepharial*   ISBN: *1-59462-308-2*   **$13.45**
In these days of advanced thinking it is a matter of common observation that we have left many of the old landmarks behind and that we are now pressing forward to greater heights and to a wider horizon than that which represented the mind-content of our progenitors...   Astrology Pages 144

Thought Vibration or The Law of Attraction in the Thought World   ISBN: *1-59462-127-6*   **$12.95**

by William Walker Atkinson   Psychology/Religion Pages 144

Optimism *by Helen Keller*   ISBN: *1-59462-108-X*   **$15.95**
Helen Keller was blind, deaf, and mute since 19 months old, yet famously learned how to overcome these handicaps, communicate with the world, and spread her lectures promoting optimism. An inspiring read for everyone...   Biographies/Inspirational Pages 84

Sara Crewe *by Frances Burnett*   ISBN: *1-59462-360-0*   **$9.45**
In the first place, Miss Minchin lived in London. Her home was a large, dull, tall one, in a large, dull square, where all the houses were alike, and all the sparrows were alike, and where all the door-knockers made the same heavy sound...   Childrens/Classic Pages 88

The Autobiography of Benjamin Franklin *by Benjamin Franklin*   ISBN: *1-59462-135-7*   **$24.95**
The Autobiography of Benjamin Franklin has probably been more extensively read than any other American historical work, and no other book of its kind has had such ups and downs of fortune. Franklin lived for many years in England, where he was agent...   Biographies/History Pages 332

Name	
Email	
Telephone	
Address	
City, State ZIP	

☐ **Credit Card**   ☐ **Check / Money Order**

Credit Card Number	
Expiration Date	
Signature	

Please Mail to: *Book Jungle*
PO Box 2226
Champaign, IL 61825
or Fax to: *630-214-0564*

ORDERING INFORMATION
web: *www.bookjungle.com*
email: *sales@bookjungle.com*
fax: *630-214-0564*
mail: *Book Jungle PO Box 2226 Champaign, IL 61825*
or PayPal *to sales@bookjungle.com*

Please contact us for bulk discounts

DIRECT-ORDER TERMS

20% Discount if You Order Two or More Books
Free Domestic Shipping!
Accepted: Master Card, Visa, Discover, American Express

www.ingramcontent.com/pod-product-compliance
Lightning Source LLC
Chambersburg PA
CBHW081232090426
42738CB00016B/3263